THE AMERICAN HOUSE TODAY

THE AMERICAN
HOUSE TODAY

*In fond memory of Afsoon Behzad,
for her wholehearted love, friendship and support.*
                              Arian Mostaedi

Author: *Arian Mostaedi*
Publishers: *Carles Broto & Josep Mª Minguet*

Editorial team:
Projects Manager: *Soledad Lorenzo*
Production & Graphic Design: *Francisco Orduña*
Graphic & Layout Design: *Fernando Graells*
Architectural Adviser: *Maria Ribas*
Text: *Marta Alcaraz*
Editorial Coordinator: *Cristina Soler*
Editorial Assistant: *Tania Gibernau*

© Carles Broto i Comerma
Caspe, 46 4º E
08010 BARCELONA
Tel.: 34 93 301 21 99
Fax: 34 93 301 00 21

ISBN: 84-89861-37-4

Printed in Spain. 2002

No part of this publication may be reproduced, stored in a retrieval system or transmitted in any form or means, electronic, mechanical, photocopying, recording or otherwise, without the prior written permission of the owner of the Copyright.

THE AMERICAN HOUSE TODAY

linksinternational

Introduction 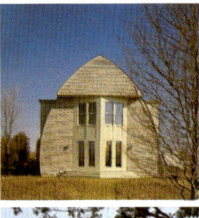 **8**

Richard **Meier**  **10** Rachofksy House

Tod **Williams**
Billie **Tsien**  **20** Rifkind House

Scogim, Elam & Bray  **30** Mountain House

Kramer E. **Woodard** Architects  **40** Highbridge - The Yanni Residence

Rick **Joy**  **50** Palmer Residence

Hut Sachs Studio  **60** Divney Loft

Susan T. **Rodríguez**  **68** Island Cabin

William H. **Grover**
Centerbrook Architects
& Planners  **78** House in Southern Connecticut

Dennis **Wedlick** Architect  **84** Katz House

Linda **Searl**
Joseph **Valerio**

94
Ohio House

Vincent **Ashbahian**

102
Siegal Penthouse

Moneo Brock Studio

110
Tribeca Home and Studio

Charles **Gwathmey**
Robert **Siegel**

120
San Onofre Residence

Cheng Design

128
Hogan / Mayo Residence

Hariri & Hariri Architects

136
Riverbend House

Hanrahan & Meyers

146
Kern Apartment / Moma Tower

Joel **Sanders** Architect

154
Apartment on Central Park West

Roger **Hirsch**
Susan **Frostén**
Drew **Souza**

160
Fire Island House

Will **Bruder**

170
Byrne Residence

introduction

introduction

In the second third of the 20th century, the political and social turmoil in Europe led many great architects to move to the United States, where they could develop and try out many of their ideas. The emigration of some of the most important representatives of the Modern Movement contributed to the international dissemination of their move away from historicism and arts and crafts tendencies, and led them to consider different architectural traditions, vernacular techniques and a new reality far removed from the European one. America was the Brave New World, the nearest thing to a tabula rasa on which they could imagine, create and build free of limitations and academicism. Europe and America came together in a country where figures such as Mies van der Rohe, Gropius, Breuer and Frank Lloyd Wright converged. While Europe declined, the United States flourished, and the construction of dwellings offered the architects the possibility of experimenting in a country without complexes and without the burden of a cultural legacy that would hinder their creativity. Due to the characteristics of the dwelling, which have always made it very attractive for the development of innovative concepts, it became a testing ground for new sensibilities.

At the turn of the century, the dwelling conserves its capacity of seduction more than ever, a more discreet attraction than that of spectacular public works, but an equally stimulating one. The house is a refuge, a place that we occupy, that we inhabit, and above all a place for living. Our personality impregnates every corner of our home ineffably, endowing it with meaning. However, this is a two-way movement: the house transforms us, it models us quiet and subtly; and the architect succumbs to the temptation of contributing to the construction of this personal world.

Mack Scogin states that the house is "the greatest experiment in American architecture". But a canonical model synthesising the characteristics of the dwelling in the United States, The American house, does not exist. The United States is not a uniform, homogeneous whole but a conglomerate of cultures, traditions and influences that has been built, and is still being built, thanks to the contributions of people from all over the world. And its architecture could not escape this melting pot. In this book we explore American houses. Nineteen projects by consecrated and emerging figures propose creative, stimulating and even challenging solutions to the complex art of inhabiting and show us that life still goes on after 1945. One of the characteristics of contemporary American architecture is investigation, mixture and revision: investigation and mixture of materials and construction techniques, revision of styles and typologies. After the technological boom of the eighties and the pragmatism of the nineties, one can detect a certain nostalgia for the major tendencies of the century, and a desire to reinterpret them and to renew their postulates.

Each of the works chosen presents a revision of conceived precepts. The house is a subject for redefinition, for experiment. The architects seek effective, singular, ecological (one of the key concepts of the architecture of the new century) and functional formulas that respond to the needs of the inhabitants.

Through such varied proposals as the revision of the Modern Movement by Tod Williams and Billie Tsien, the organic work of Rick Joy, the exercise of applied geometry by Roger Hirsch, the recycling of vernacular typologies by Dennis Wedlick and the immaculate constructions of Richard Meier and of Gwathmey and Siegel, this book offers an interesting panorama of American architecture today, and of the dwelling as the expression of its vitality.

Richard Meier
Rachofksy House
Dallas, Texas

Set in a suburban landscape, this house/private museum is anchored to the ground by a podium faced in black granite that extends both in front of and behind the main body of the building. The white form of the house hovers on piles above the podium like an opaque plane, pierced by a number of discrete openings. A succession of spatial layers recedes from this taut surface to accommodate the house's principal volumes. The metal-faced front elevation that shields the living volume gives way on the north and west elevations to taut curtain walls that, together with the opaque front, inflect the interior layered space toward a small body of water to the southwest. Two sheets of water a reflection pool and a swimming pool penetrate the podium at the rear of the house. The swimming pool, plus a cubic pool house and a low wall, effectively terminate the sitework at the western end.

Two separate stairs provide access to the three floors of the house: an enclosed spiral stair to the south and an open switchback stair to the north. This contrast between private and public circulation is echoed consistently in the organization of the volumes within. Thus, the public stair opening off the gallery foyer leads directly to the double-height living room on the first floor, while the cylindrical private stair ascends to the guest suite and library on the second floor and the master suite on the floor above. Two separate volumes on the third floor, a suspended study and an excercise room, afford vews of the living volume and the garden. All glass walls that are exposed to low-angle western light are protected by electrically operated venetian blinds.

A ramped stair giving access from the swimming pool, a dog-leg stair to the roof terrace, and a two-car garage lodged under the guest suite on the south side of the house complete the symmetrical repertoire. The exterior of the house is clad in white enameled aluminium panels with aluminum fenestration and insulated glazing.

■ Scott Frances/ESTO Photographics

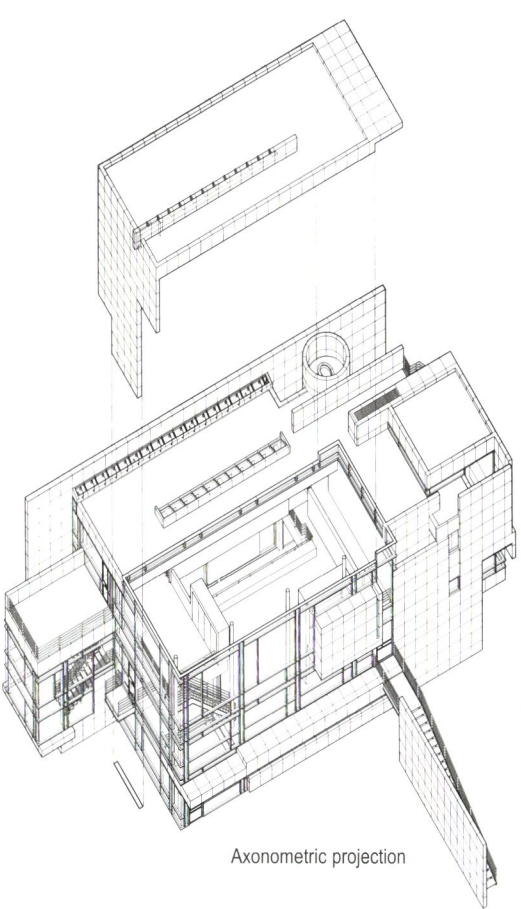

Axonometric projection

Site plan

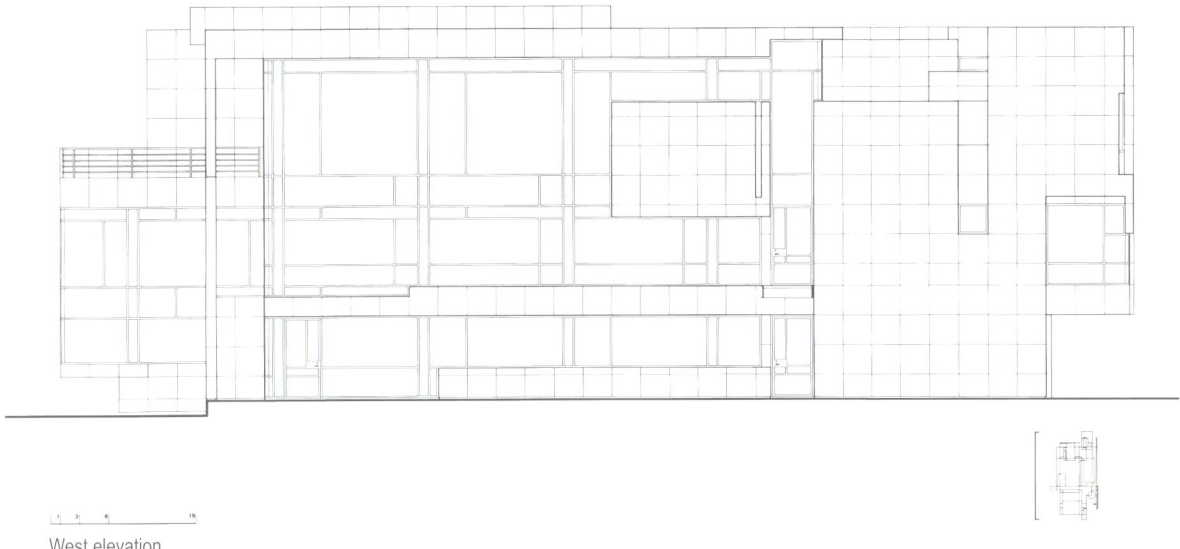

West elevation

The stairways set the pace for both the building's interior and exterior. A metal structure following the progression of the wall provides access from the garden.

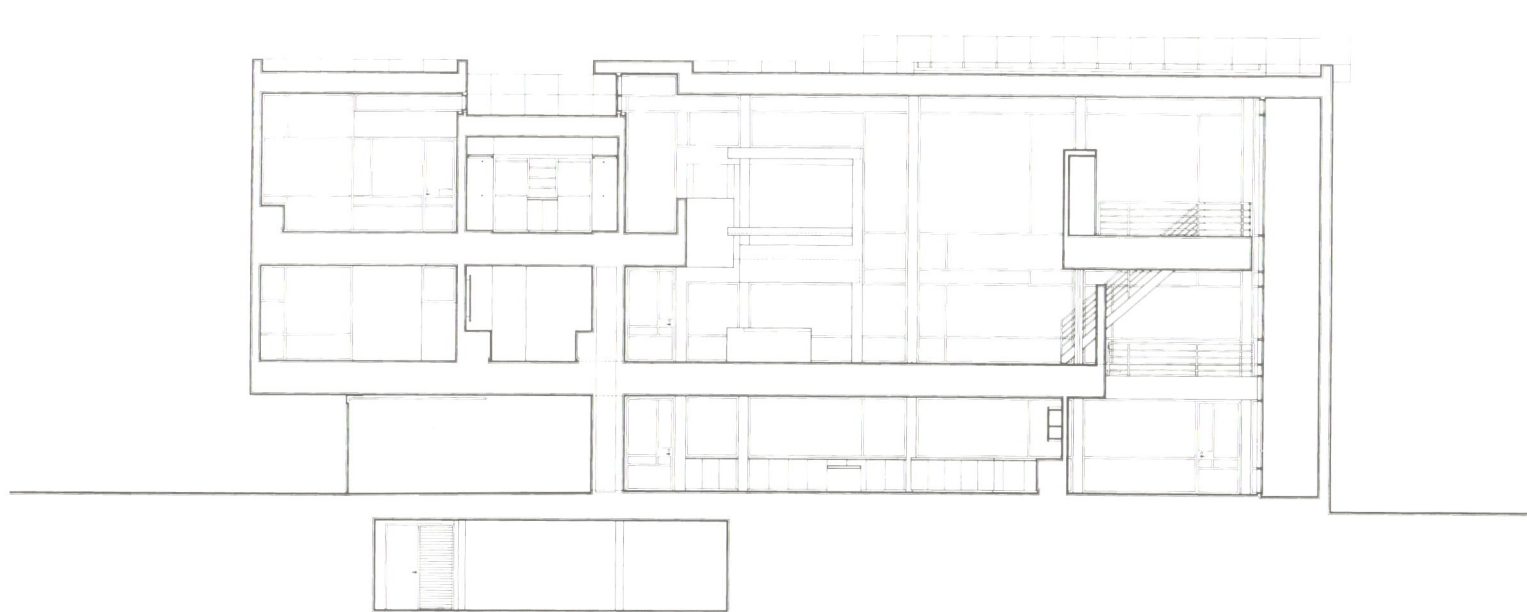

Section to the west

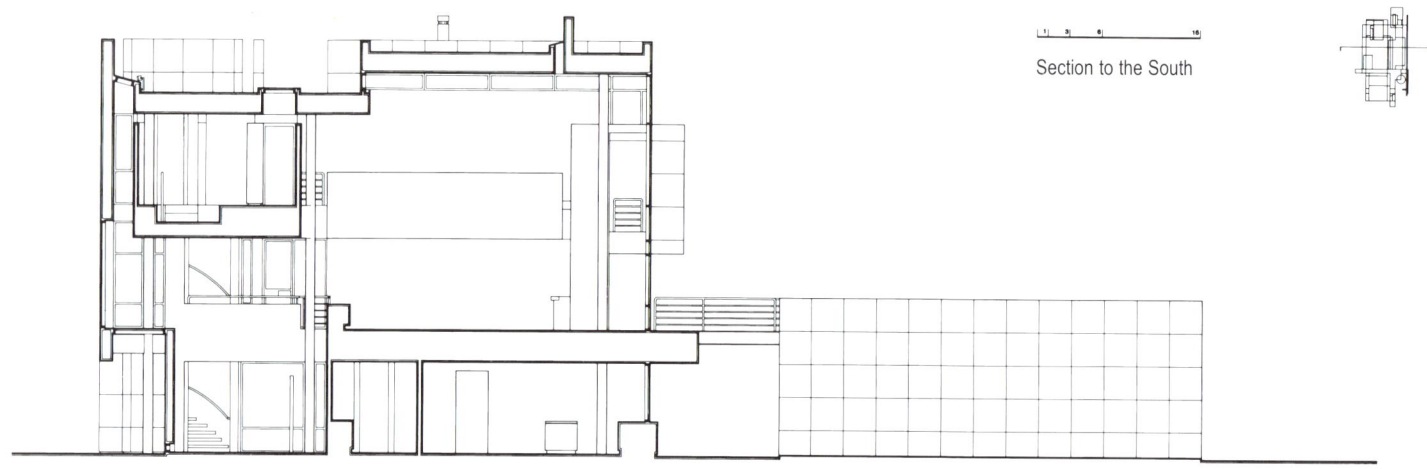

Section to the South

First floor plan

Second floor plan

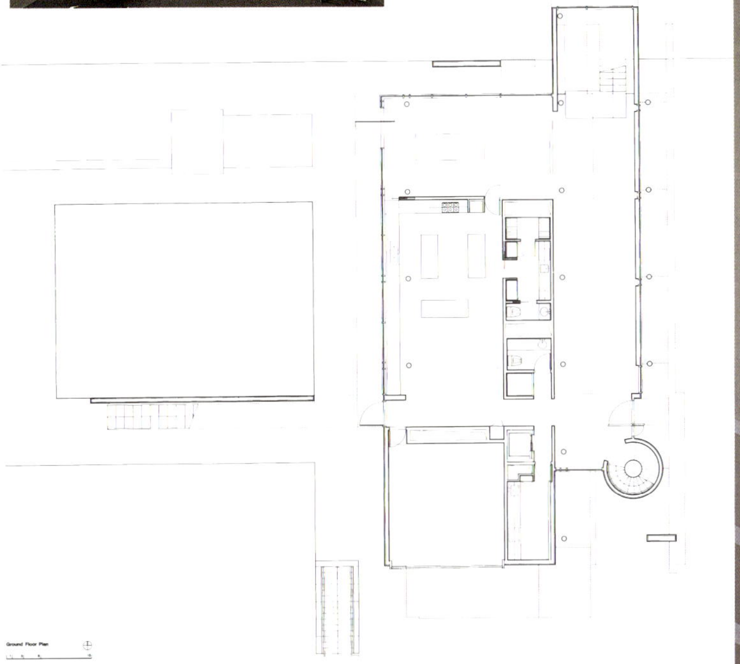

Ground floor plan

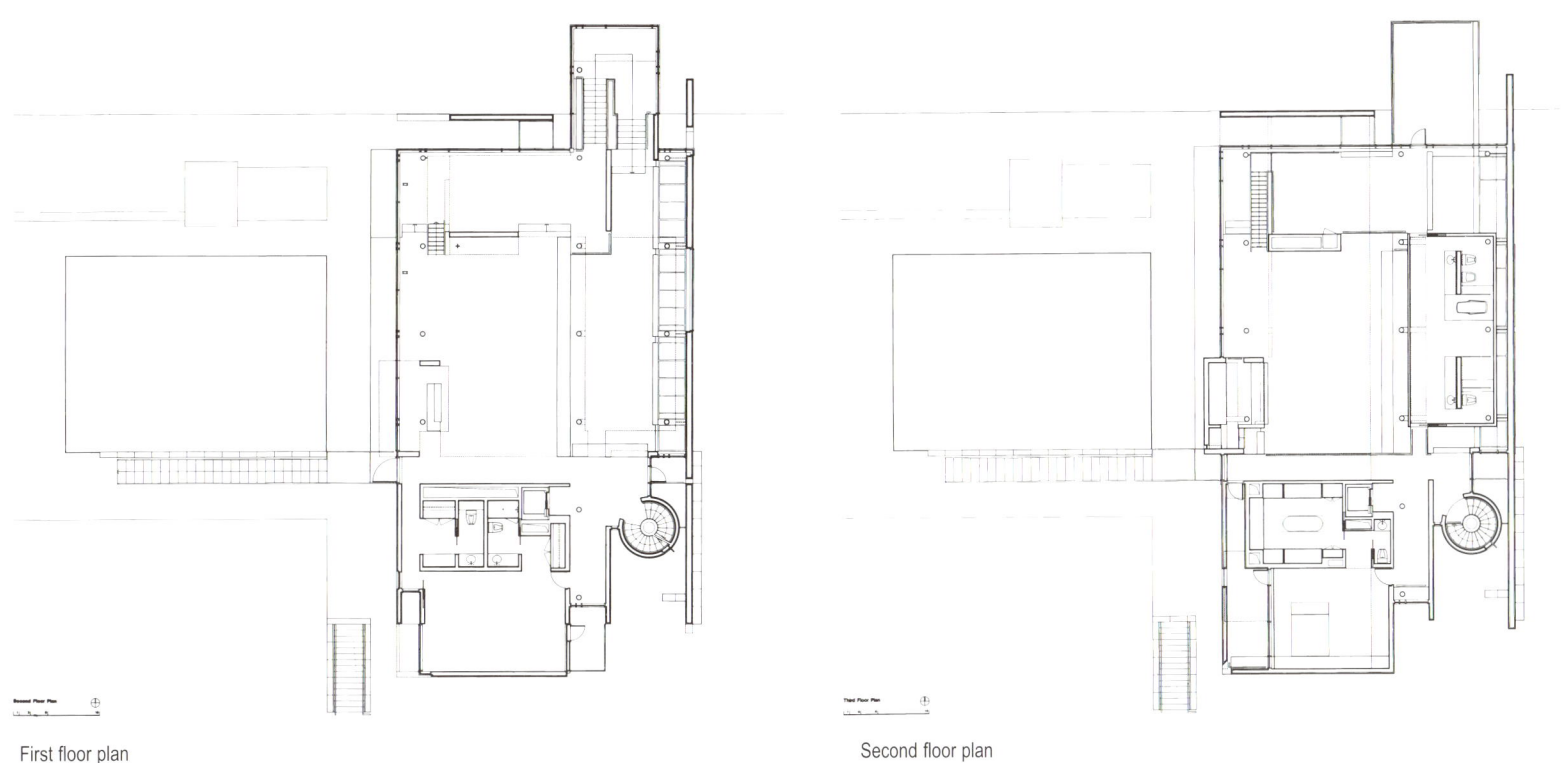

The colour white, used to full effect to coat the building´s exterior, plays an important role in the design. It competes with the verdure of the surroundings and acts as a canvas for the daily and seasonal changes of light.

Tod Williams, Billie Tsien
Rifkind House

Long Island, New York

For the owners it is their first house. As professionals with grown children and life long city dwellers who have never owned a car or a house, the design and construction of this house has had great significance. It is to serve as a weekend retreat, a place for them both to work and a compound for the children, spouses and future grandchildren. It is to be a place apart; an antidote to the intensity of their lives in New York, a refuge in which to enjoy their desire for peace and quiet.

The site by a pond and with distant views of the ocean is approached on foot because the parking has been pulled away from the house. Organized in three volumes on one level, one enters a courtyard suggested by the placement of the buildings. The house is not air-conditioned but takes advantage of cross-breezes and a site which has beautiful pitch pines and complete separation from any neighbors.

The three pavilions describe the programme and they have been configured so that each room frames a different view. Each room and bedroom has its own entrance to the landscape. The central block contains at its centre the kitchen with living room on one side and dining on the other, and a small reading loft above. The master bedroom, dressing bath and study are separate and may be occupied independently from the third block which may also be occupied independently. This third block contains three bedrooms for children and guests. A smaller volume is a panting/storage and refuse shed.

The house is wood frame with cedar siding and Douglas fir lining the interior of solid exterior walls. Windows are mahogany. Floors are Douglas fir and New York bluestone in honed and split face, as is the chimney. Built-in bookshelves, beds, dressers and custom furniture are American cherry.

The architect«s desire was to design a house which finds its place and meaning though a careful choreography with the existing trees, balancing form and nature. Its integral relationship to the landscape and light allows the house with transform over the course of a day and the season.

Michael Moran

The pavilions that form the dwelling are distributed on the site in a very rational way. Their layout guarantees the maximum use of natural light.

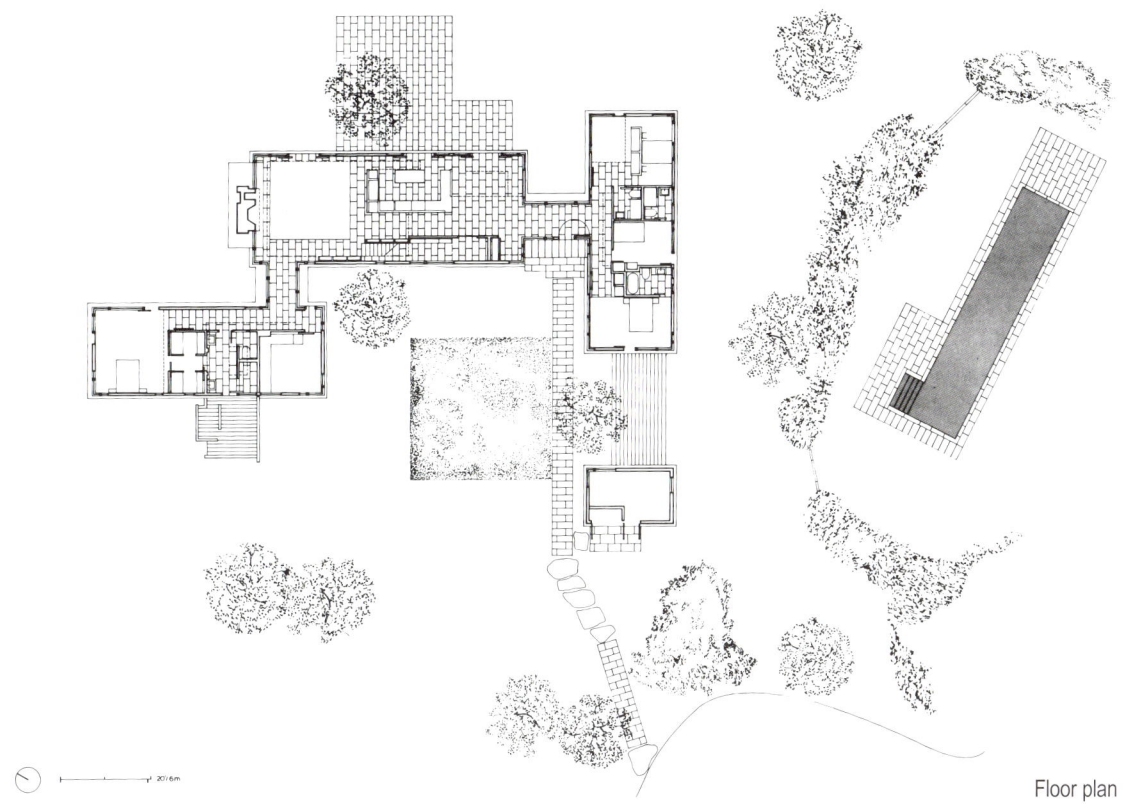

Floor plan

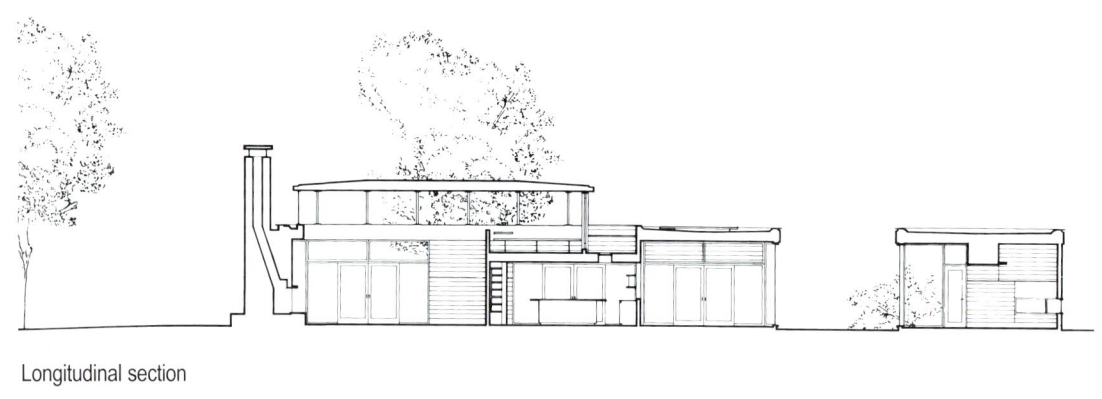

Longitudinal section

The central volume that houses the public areas of the house has a glazed facade that permits total communication between interior and exterior. The lantern windows accentuate the verticality of the space and establish a rhythm in the living room.

Scogim, Elam & Bray
Mountain House

Dillard, Georgia

From the city galleries and studios he collects regional art with the same care and affection that she gathers the wildflowers of their north Georgia site. The site and the house respond to dual interests. The site —remote private and rugged— is tucked into the foothills of the Appalachian Mountains overlooking the pasture of the Hambridge Center, a not-for-profit artist's retreat.

At the house the screen porche vies with the living room for prominence. The two spaces, outdoor/indoor, reside in a state of equivalence, happily. The generous arrival courtyard, square and stone-clad, lets onto the vertical space of the entrance gallery and visually onto the corridor gallery. It is the first interior space of the house.

The structure aspires to sustain a dialogue about the relationship of the natural to the manmade and the joys and wonders of both. Horizontal lines slice the round, softly arching and curving mountain forms. Wonderfully vertical poplar trunks are frame cut, celebrated. Used now as a weekend retreat, the house will eventually become the first house. A small guest room detached from the house provides privacy and community.

The house proper has one bedroom. Building area: 4,095 square feet. The frame is wood and steel with reinforced concrete walls defining and punctuating the rectilinear geometry. The house is clad in stucco, redwood and glass. The windows are redwood, the doors are mahogany, and the flooring is wood. The entrance courtyard is paved with rock pulled from a stream.

Timothy Hursley

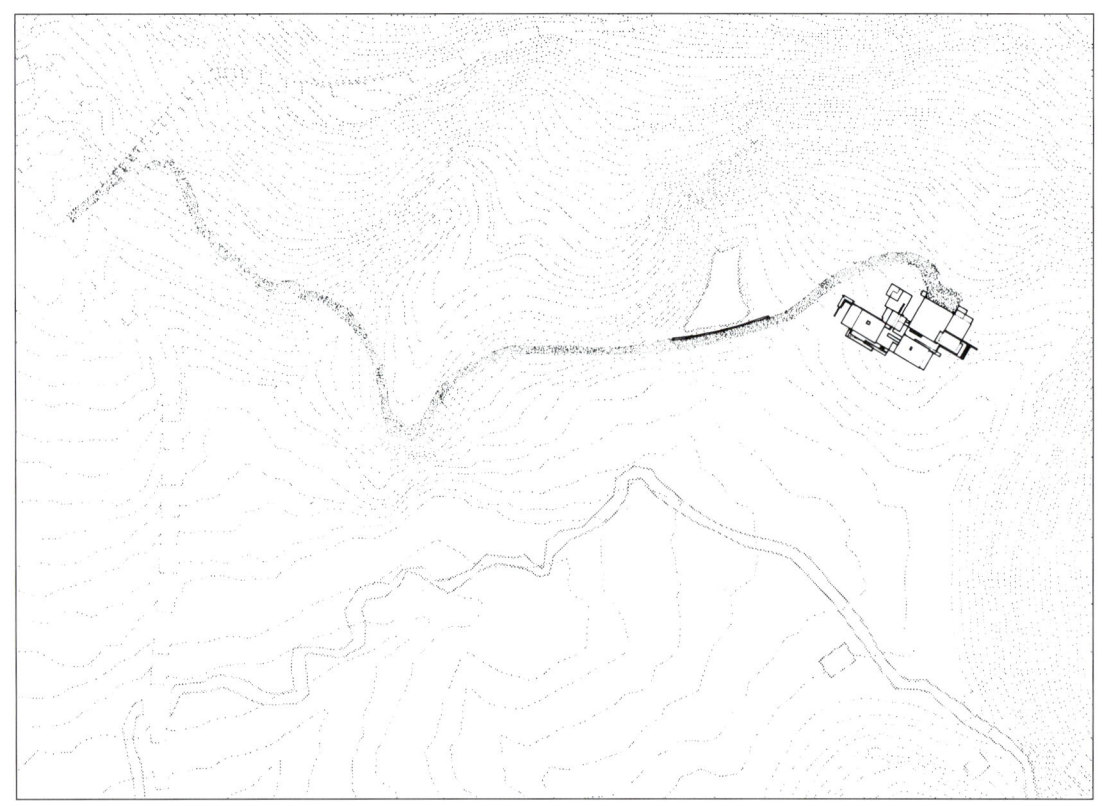

Site plan

The project is defined by the highly horizontal geometry of the construction. Besides suggesting the interior programme —rational and practical division of the atmospheres, spaciousness and a great sensation of freedom—, the horizontal lines establish a dialogue with the vertical trunks of the surrounding trees. The relationship with the landscape is not mimetic but compensatory.

The single-storey dwelling is arranged to form a square courtyard. The courtyard becomes another living space, reinforcing the idea of dialogue and interrelation between interior and exterior.

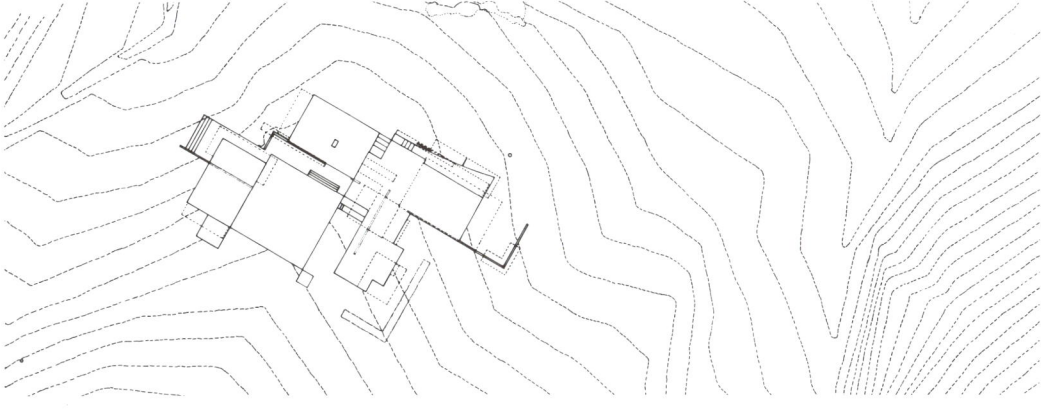

The glazed porch is a fundamental element of the dwelling. Its structure of wooden posts and beams has been left exposed, in an artificial recreation of the exterior forest.

1. Garage
2. Guest room
3. Screened porch
4. Entry
5. Gallery
6. Bedroom
7. Office
8. Kitchen
9. Pantry
10. Dining room
11. Living room
12. Inglenook
13. Outdoor room

Floor plan

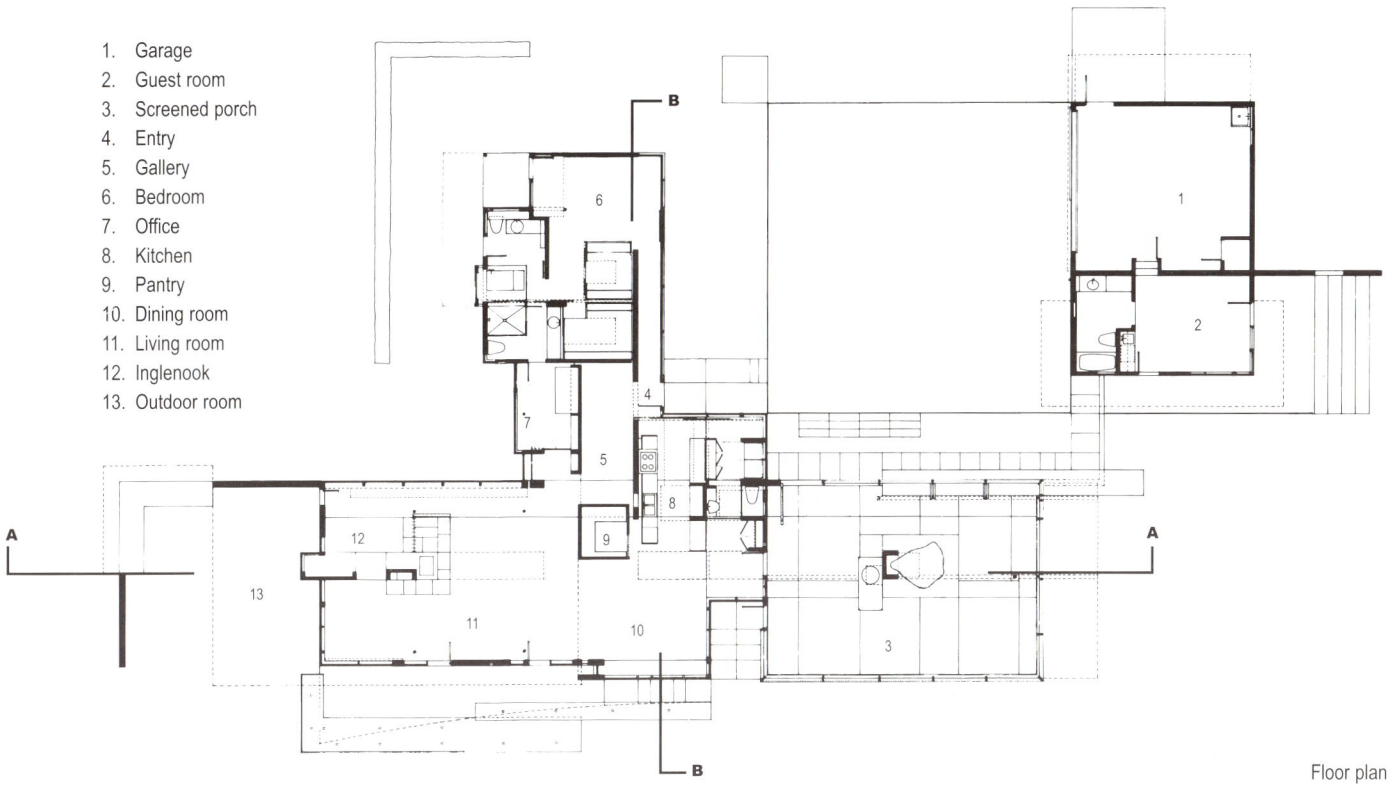

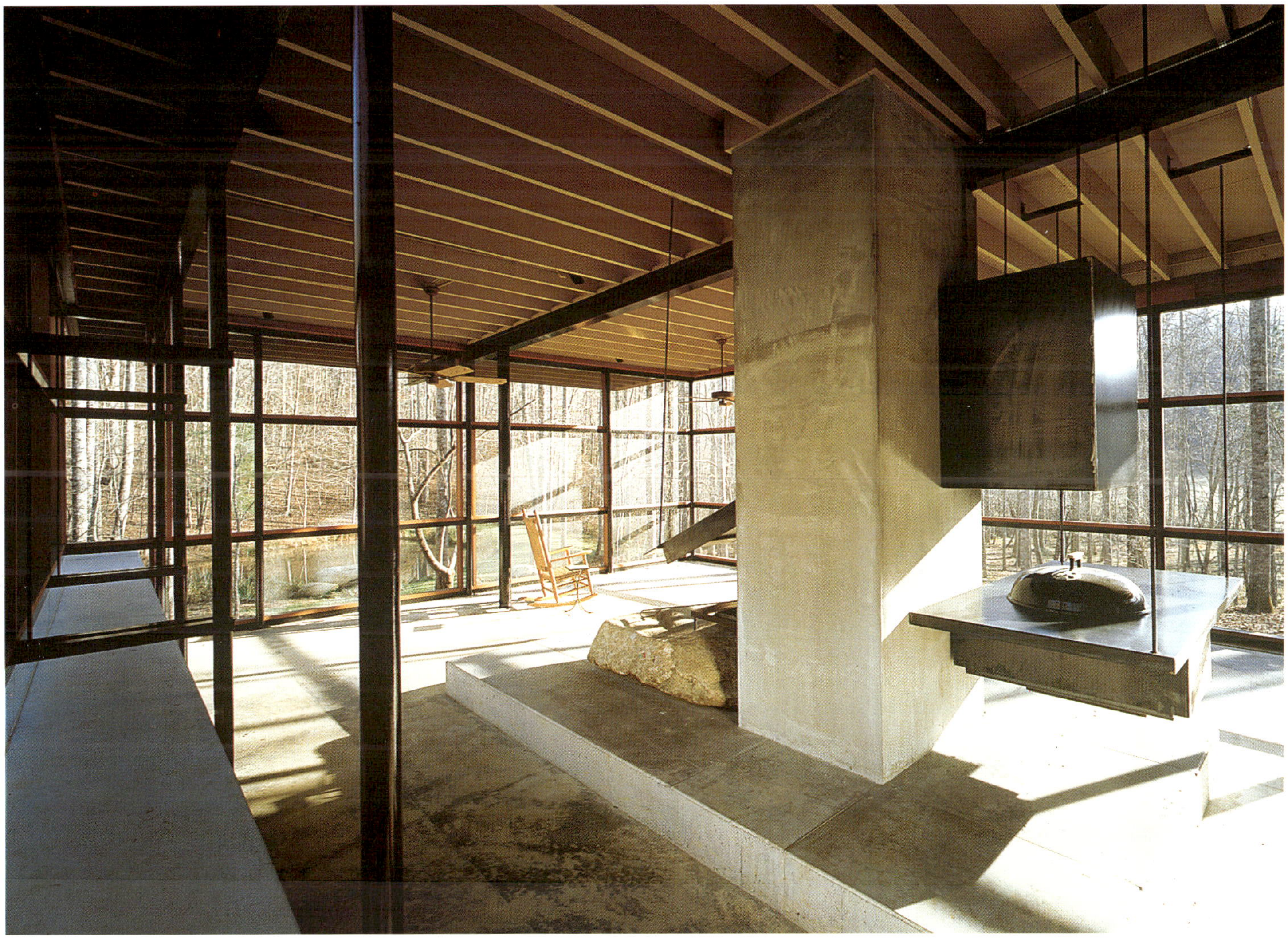

A concrete wall in the kitchen area conceals the sliding door that provides access to the pantry. It also contrasts with the colour and the texture of the wood of the flooring and the kitchen.
Rather than a space itself, the latter can be considered as an element in the house.

Section BB

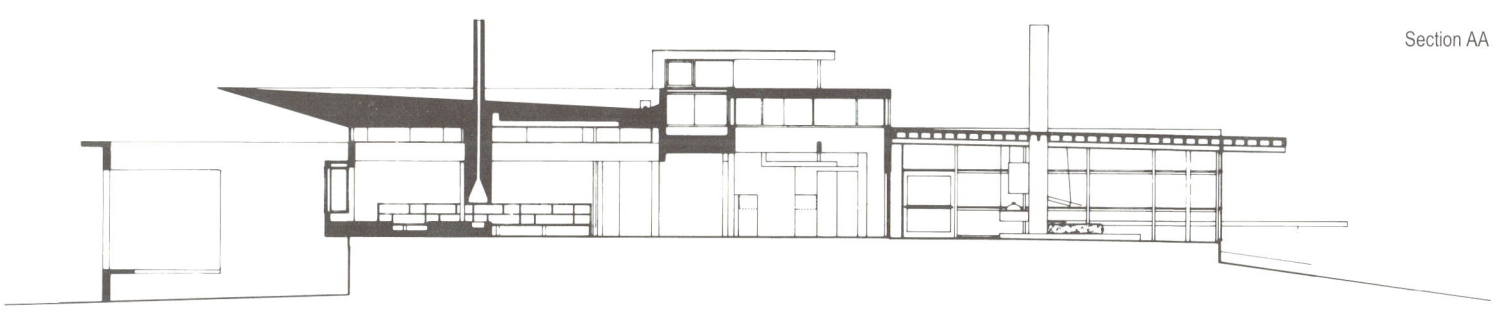

Section AA

Kramer E. Woodard Architects
Highbridge-The Yanni Residence
High Bridge, New Jersey

This residence stands on a site of 2.2 acres in Hunterdon County, a rural area of the state of New Jersey. The client, an executive, was looking for a first residence because he only spends the weekends in New York. The architects thus attempted to create a flowing, dynamic space in consonance with the environment and with its owner's needs.

The 3,000 square feet of floor area are distributed in a volume created by two parallelepipedal volumes, one of which is slightly set back from the other. This double volume is in turn developed on two levels communicated by several staircases. Parallel walls clad in pressed wood panels organize the interior distribution of the dwelling, defining spaces closed by large windows on the north and south faces. The effect is one of transparent spaces contained between walls, in a visual interplay of transparent and opaque elements.

A staircase parallel to the garage on the east side leads to the living room, the dining room and the kitchen, which share the same transparent space. Continuing toward the east there is a suite and two bedrooms separated from the living area by glass screens. On the north and south faces, two long narrow volumes run parallel to the main ones and house a bathroom, the service lift and the machine room to the north, and the main bathroom, a wardrobe of the suite and a toilet to the south.

To the west, the house opens onto the forest with wood-covered terraces. The basement level under the bedrooms houses two garages, the service lift and a storage space. The load-bearing walls receive the same chromatic treatment inside the dwelling as on the outside, a black that contrasts with the gentle surrounding colours. The vertical wall faces are painted white. Wood was used for the floors. In this scheme the architects combined balance and dynamism, with pure geometries, clear spaces and a maximum use of natural light and views of the forest.

◻ Kevin Chu / Catherine Tighe Bogert

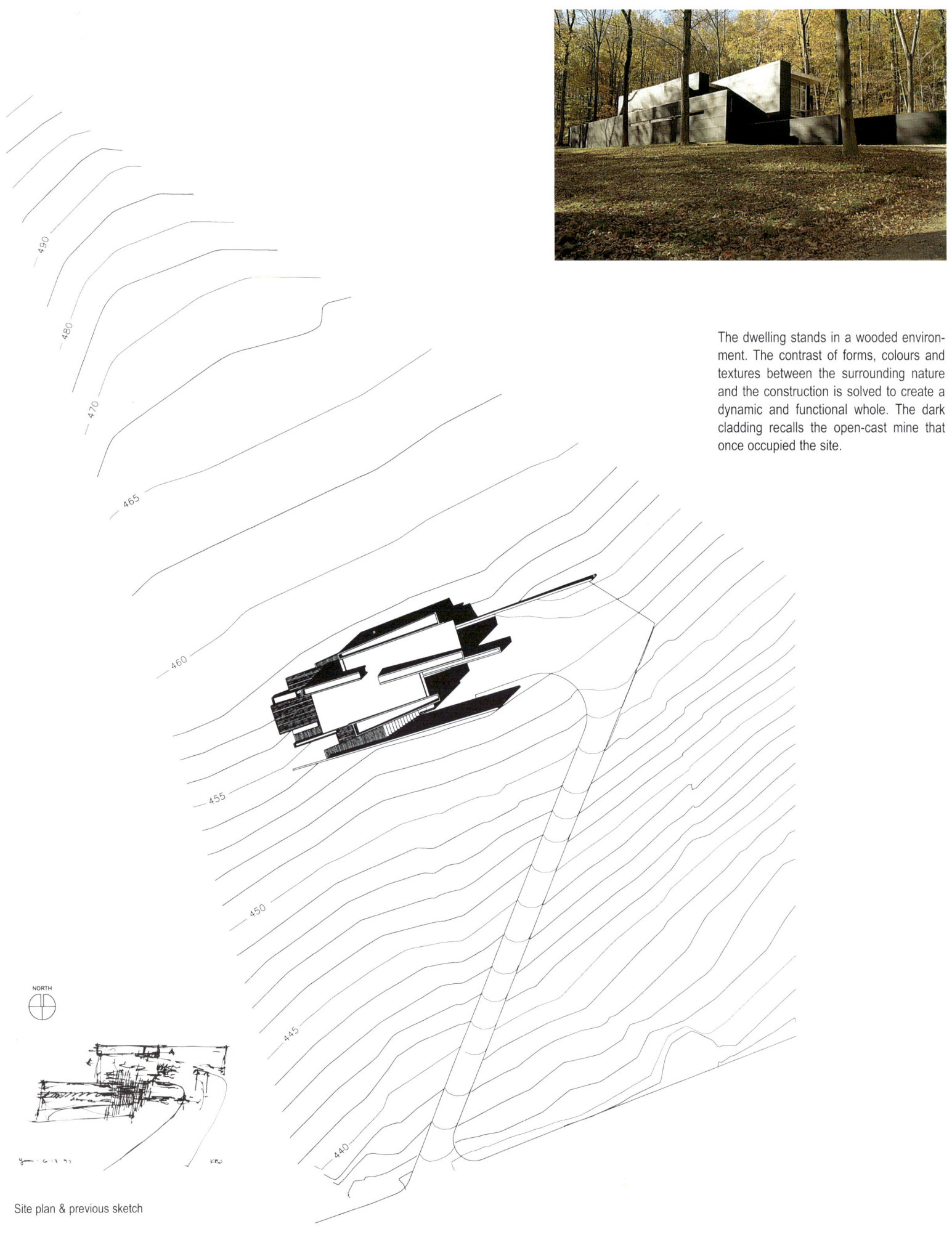

The dwelling stands in a wooded environment. The contrast of forms, colours and textures between the surrounding nature and the construction is solved to create a dynamic and functional whole. The dark cladding recalls the open-cast mine that once occupied the site.

Site plan & previous sketch

Upper level plan

1. Entry
2. Kitchen
3. Washroom
4. Living room
5. Dining room
6. Master bedroom
7. Bath
8. Laundry
9. Dumbwaiter
10. Bedroom A
11. Bedrroom B
12. Closet
13. Terrace
14. Shelves
15. Storage
16. Garage A
17. Mechanical closet
18. Garage B
19. Dumbwaiter
20. Planter
21. Driveway

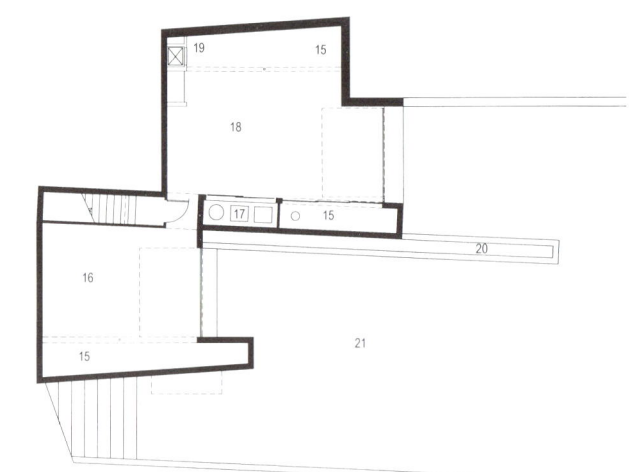

Lower level plan

A staircase located on the east facade forms the access to the dwelling. The interplay of light and shade, with shadows that are cast onto the polished surface of the walls, adds an organic dimension to the building.

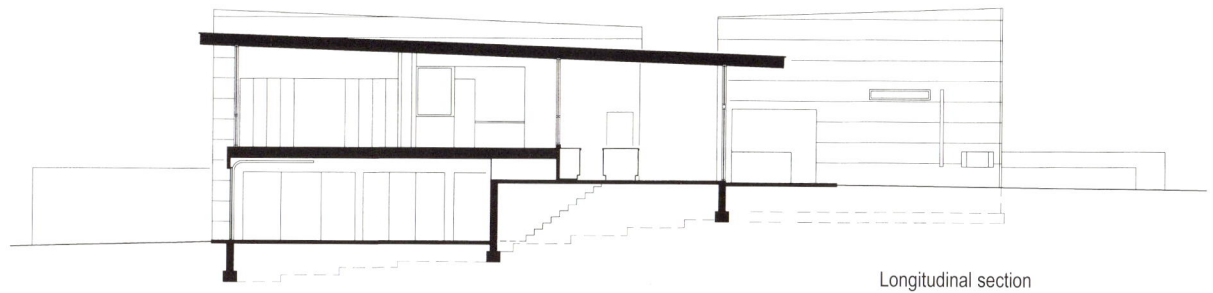

Longitudinal section

Cross-section

Inside the dwelling, the contrast between black and white on the vertical walls contributes to a better regulation of the illumination. A strategic arrangement of windows gives the space great width and a sensation of continuity between the different rooms.

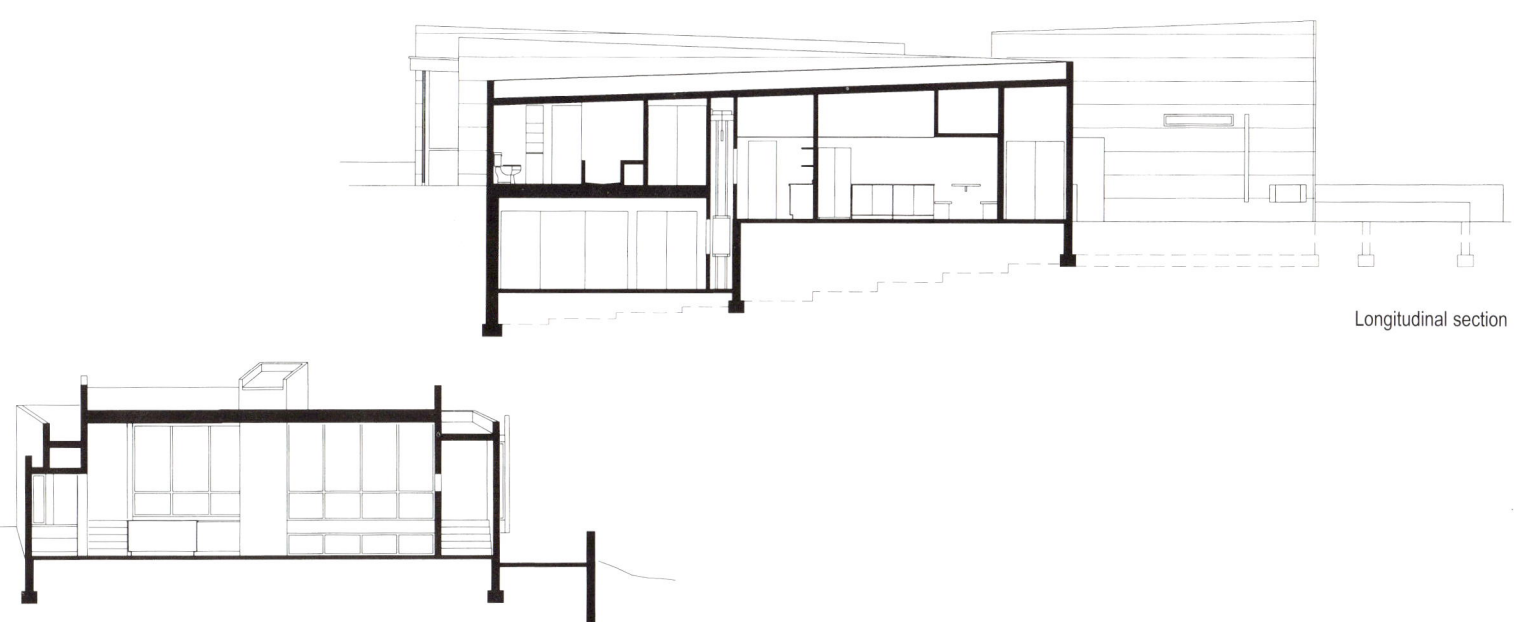

Longitudinal section

Cross-section

The house is articulated around the load-bearing walls that govern the distribution of the different areas of the dwelling and give the space a very clear rhythm. The sensation of movement is also achieved thanks to the use of primary colours.

Rick Joy
Palmer Residence
Tucson, Arizona

Rick Joy was the architect chosen by John Palmer and Annabel Rose to undertake the project for their residence in Tuscon, Arizona. Set in the lower foothills of the Catalina Mountains in north Tuscon, the site rests on the edge of a major arroyo and is lush with Sonoran Desert flora and fauna. Major views are to the north and slightly east with the dramatic Catalinas rising to over 7,000 feet above the site and only 3 miles away. The residence is set about 25 feet below the road and is almost completely obscured from view by the hillside and vegetation.

The 2,500-square foot house is divided into clearly defined "wings" separating the general living areas from the private. The first houses the bedroom, bathroom, spa and studio or "den." In the second wing we find the lobby, living room, kitchen and pantry as well as a 450-square foot porch. A separate 1400-square foot pavilion comprises a garage, shop and guest house. The resulting geometries look like rectangular boxes topped with butterfly-like roofing.

The owners requested rammed earth walls for the general structure. The house will be the primary home, a place for entertaining large groups and a respite from the couple's complicated schedules. The design was developed through a careful study of the existing vegetation and the large staying areas required for the construction of rammed earth walls. The natural surroundings have been scrupulously respected; no trees or cactus were destroyed and only one additional tree was planted.

The structure of the buildings is unreinforced rammed earth walls on concrete stem walls and spread footings. The earth mix on this project combines soils from three different sources in the Tuscon area, chosen for the color and structural integrity and blended with a small amount of iron oxide and 3% portland cement. The walls and foundations for the house alone weigh approximately 500 tons. Weathered steel has been used to construct the roofs, exterior garage walls and miscellaneous hardware while the ceilings and doors are made of rough-sawn Douglas fir. The large window walls on the north side of the bedroom and living room are frameless reglet set insulated glass with glass mullions. The kitchen and the porch are separated by a wall of 1/2" tempered glass. A frameless glass pivot door aids circulation between the two sections.

The house will be cooled by evaporative cooling systems and heated with hot water radiant heating in the polished concrete floor slabs.

The residence is, in essence, an integrated element of the local scenery, in complete harmony with the environment, reflecting the express wishes of the owners.

◻ Bill Timmerman

Floor Plan
1. Entry
2. Living
3. Kitchen
4. Pantry
5. Porch
6. Bedroom
7. Den
8. Spa
9. Garage
10. Guest bedroom
11. Shop

One of the defining characteristics of Rick Joy is the fitting combination of different materials: the rammed earth walls, the large glazed surfaces, and the timber roofs which are then covered with corrugated iron.

The lighting of the home was manipulated so as to produce a special "chiaroscuro" effect. The different surfaces of the vertical faces (rough walls and polished timber) also help to create a subtle and ever-changing interplay of light and shadow.

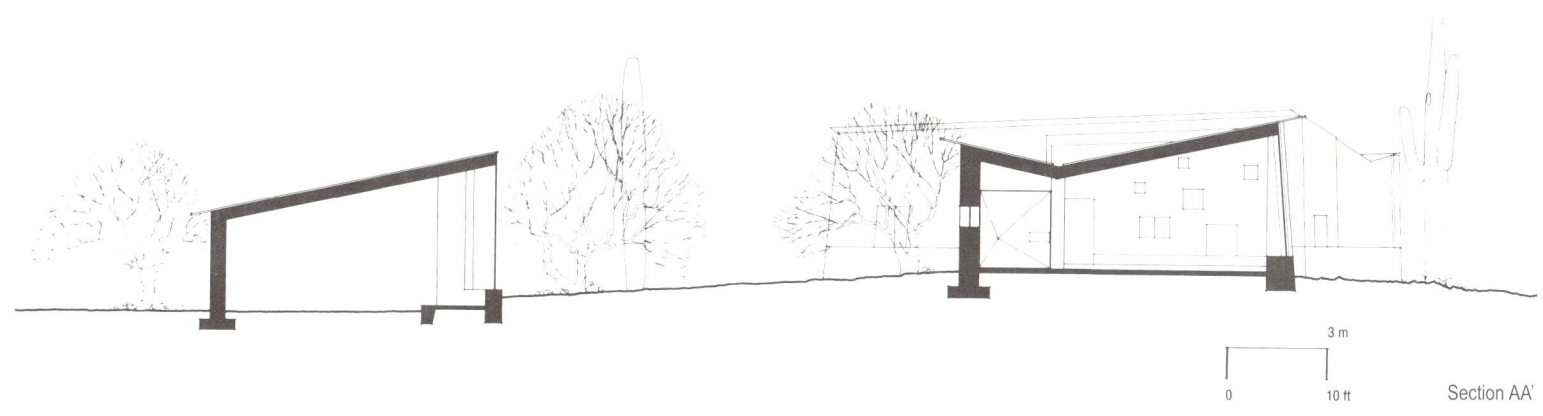

Section AA'

The large glazed surfaces of this home help to establish a fluid dialogue between interior and exterior. The building materials mirror the natural setting, as is the case with the rammed earth walls and the timber, or succeed in providing a contrast, as is the case with the corrugated iron and some of the metal furniture.

Hut Sachs Studio
Divney Loft
New York City, New York

The studio used the volume of the cherry entry cabinetry and gold leaf form of the master bathroom to divide the 2300 square ft. Soho loft into two realms: an open living, dining and kitchen area where the painted wood joists and columns of the loft are exposed, and the more private space of the master bedroom.

A glass panel in the sloped ceiling of the gold leaf form allows the existing skylight to transmit light between the master bathroom and the kitchen. Likewise, several skylights in the center of the appartment provide the correct lighting for those rooms which are spatially removed from the façade.

The client's affection for hand craftsmanship is evidenced in the handling of the materials: the use of salvaged brick in the fireplace, the pattern of cherry handles on the clear cherry cabinet faces in the kitchen, the artist tiles designed by Richard Rudich in the master bathroom and the sculpting of the cherry headboard and ceiling.

The architecture reconciles the raw New York loft space with the refined forms of the new construction by allowing each to maintain their identity.

The lightness of the walls and the sculptural forms of some of the furniture organize the dwelling spatially and allow it to be perceived as a whole.

 Jeff Goldberg/Esto Photographics

1. Entry
2. Living
3. Dining
4. Sitting Area
5. Kitchen
6. Master Bathroom
7. Bathroom
8. Master Bedroom
9. Study

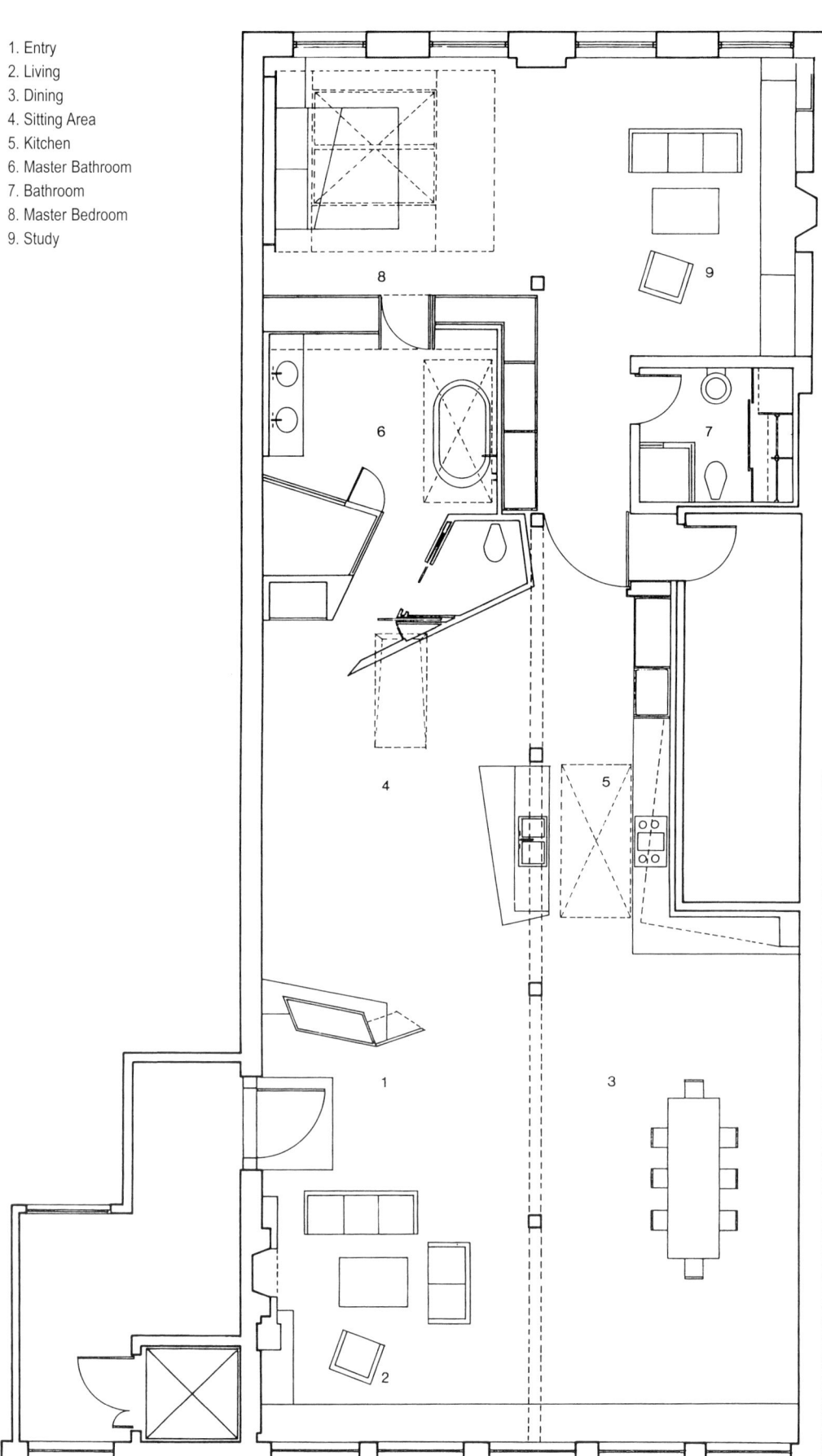

Despite the profound remodeling that was carried out, the architects managed to maintain the character of the loft intact by conserving some of its most characteristic elements such as the floor slabs, the exposed masonry walls and the heavy wooden structure.

Functionally, the dwelling is divided into two clearly differentiated spaces: a large open zone containing the living room, the dining room and the kitchen, and a more private zone containing the main bedroom.

Whereas in the more open area of the dwelling the cherry wood floors contrast with white painted exposed masonry walls, in the main bedroom wood is also used on the walls and ceilings.

67

Susan T. Rodríguez
Island Cabin

Penobscot Bay, Maine

This seasonal cabin is located on a small private island in the Penobscot Bay approximately 12 miles off the coast of Maine. The cabin is situated on a bluff overlooking a narrow nautical passage. The overall building form is composed of two simple shed roof structures joined by a raised deck and walkway. These two pitched roof structures are essential to the water collection system for the island. The larger volume opens up to the water view and the smaller one to the wooded landscape from the water, yet still allows for dramatic views from within. The detail development of the cabin is intended to animate the simple structures with shade and shadow and highlight many of the functional aspects of the design; its gutter and downspout system, bracketed roof overhang, and shutters. The primary building material for the cabin is wood. A repetitive, pre-cut post and beam structure was erected on the site in two and a half days on a pressure-treated frame base. It is enclosed with laminated decking and cedar shingles. Cedar trim elements, wood windows, pine shutters and metal detailing complete the assembly. The shutters operate on sliding barn door hardware and galvanised hinges fabricate locally. A continuous clerestory window in the larger cabin disengages the sloping roof plane from the vertical wall surface, allowing the structure to visually penetrate from interior to exterior.

The larger cabin is the main living space with sleeping accommodation on two levels and storage below. The smaller cabin provides flexible space for sleeping or recreation and houses three water cisterns below. The island has its own independent infrastructure. Propane powers the appliances and lighting, along with a small generator for pumping water and septic. A water tower, set at the island's highpoint, pressurises the system. A wood stove provides heat, when necessary during the season.

◻ Jeff Goldberg/Esto Photographics

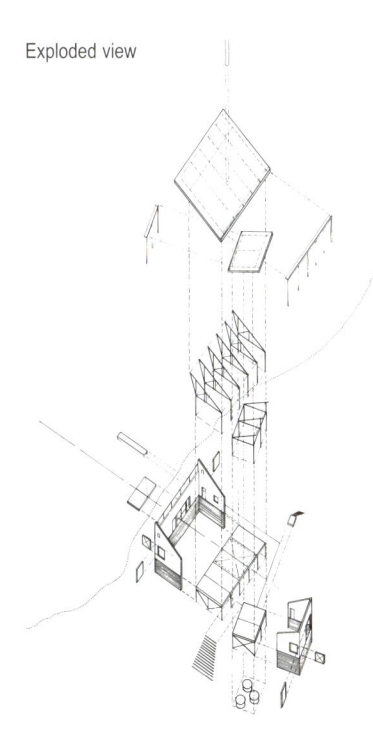

Exploded view

The design emerges in response to numerous parameters and opportunities prompted by this remote location; restricted site access, use of vernacular construction methods, alternative energy sources, a sensitivity to the natural environment, the use of rainwater to supplement a dug well, low maintenance requirements, and a short building season.

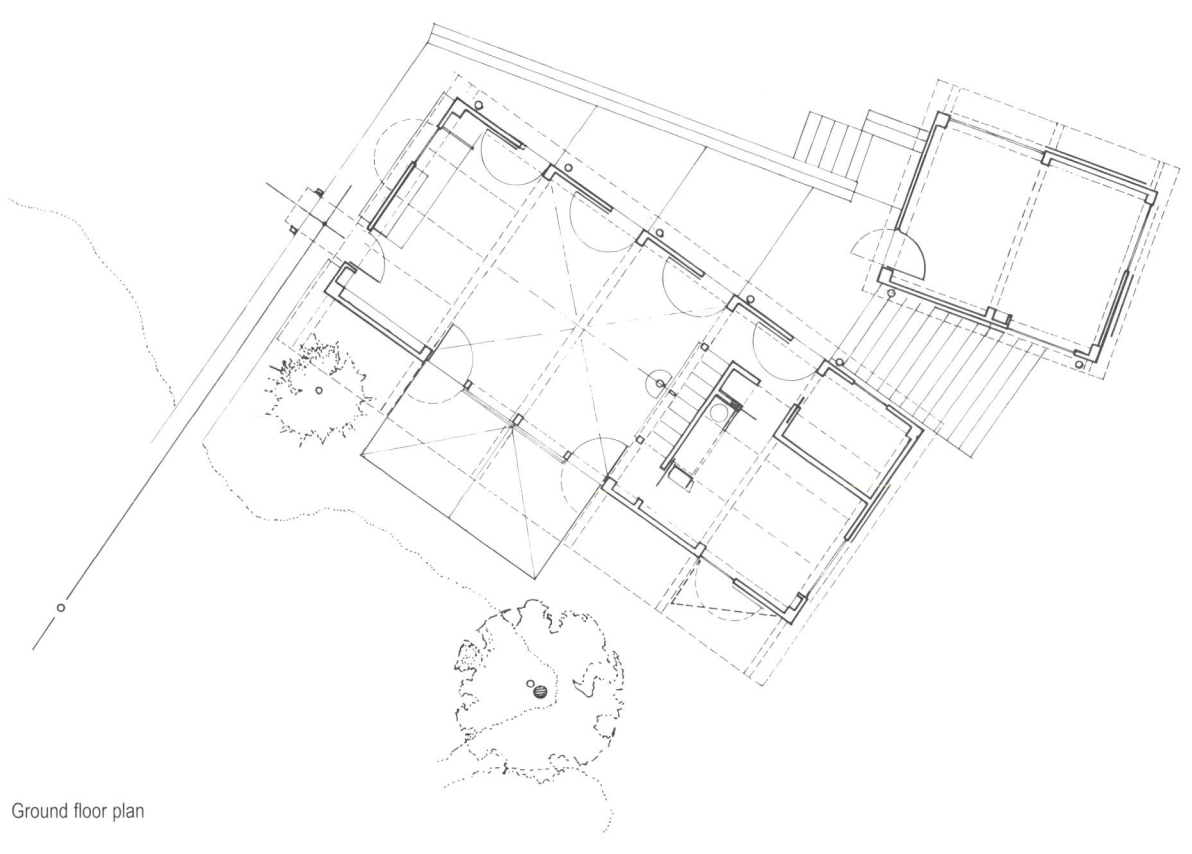

Ground floor plan

73

In keeping with the exterior character of the cabin, the interior reflects the rational structural order of the building, exposing the post and beam structure.

Perspective view

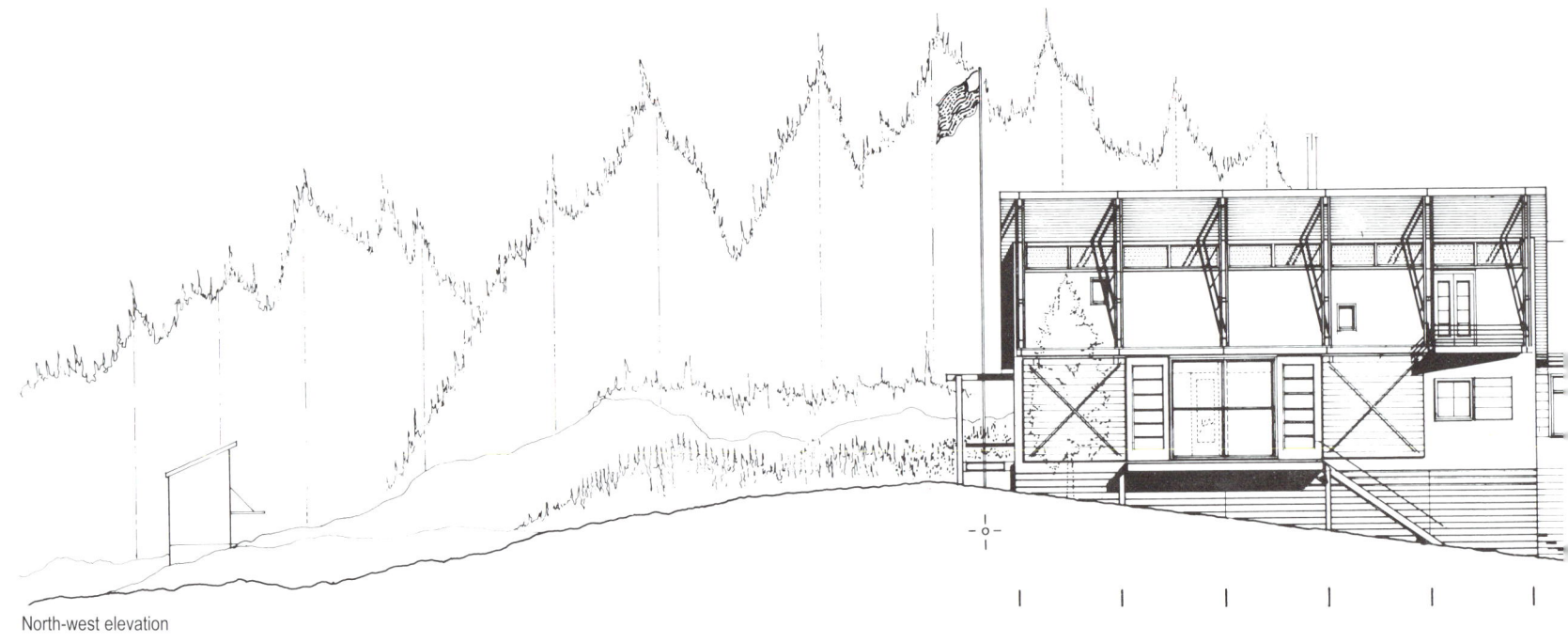

North-west elevation

76

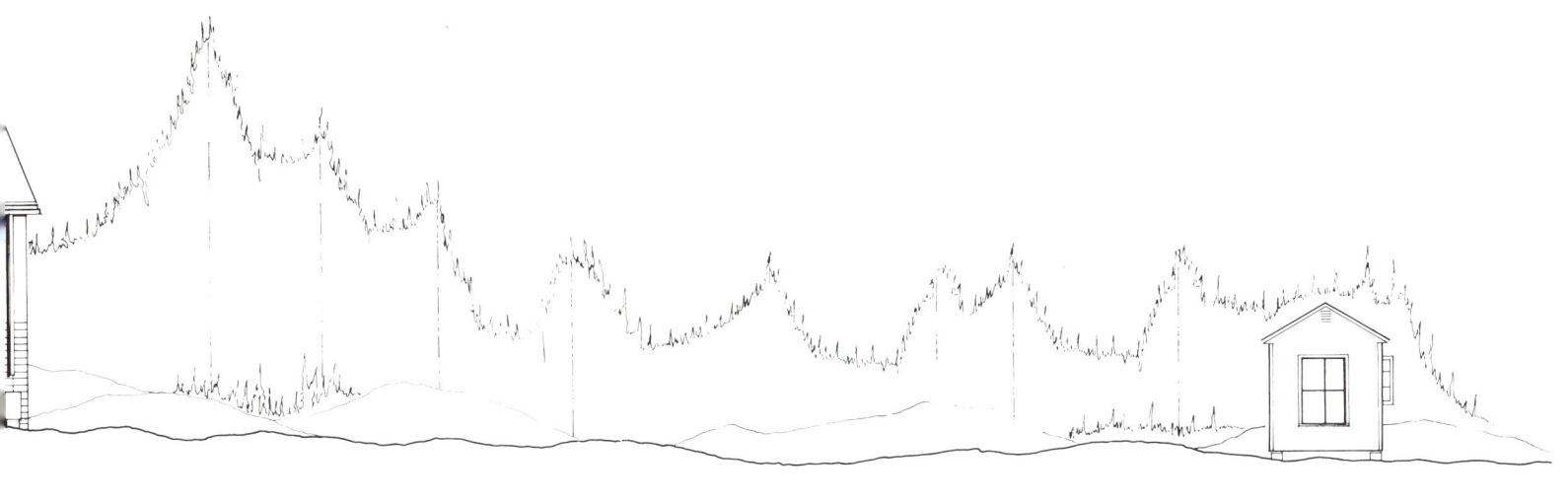

A wood stove provides heat, when necessary, during the winter season. However, it was the architect's intention to design a house which is energy-efficient. Wood is a natural isolator and "breathes" with the dwellers within. The natural weathering of the wooden structure, over time, will further integrate the structure into the natural setting.

William H. Grover, Centerbrook Architects & Planners
House in Southern Connecticut

Southern Conneticut

Originally built in the early 70's, this mostly flat-roofed house is located on a beautiful site next to a small river. The owners were tempted to demolish it due to its dark slate tile floors and overgrown landscape but since it was sturdily built, they finally decided to change its character instead. A gable roof and an attic were added to the garage, the circular driveway was transformed into a courtyard and a new storage building with the same proportions as the garage was constructed, across the courtyard, next to the entrance to the house. A two-story gable-roofed wing added two bedrooms and bathrooms. Electric radiant ceiling heat was replaced with more efficient hot water baseboard heat. A swimming pool and a terrace was located to the south near the kitchen and family room. A new steel-framed wood deck replaced the narrow walkway facing the river. Overgrown landscape was cut back or removed. This is an example of recycling an out-of-date endangered house into an energy-efficient home that fits more comfortably into its site and its community.

© Jeff Goldberg/Esto Photografics

Upper floor plan

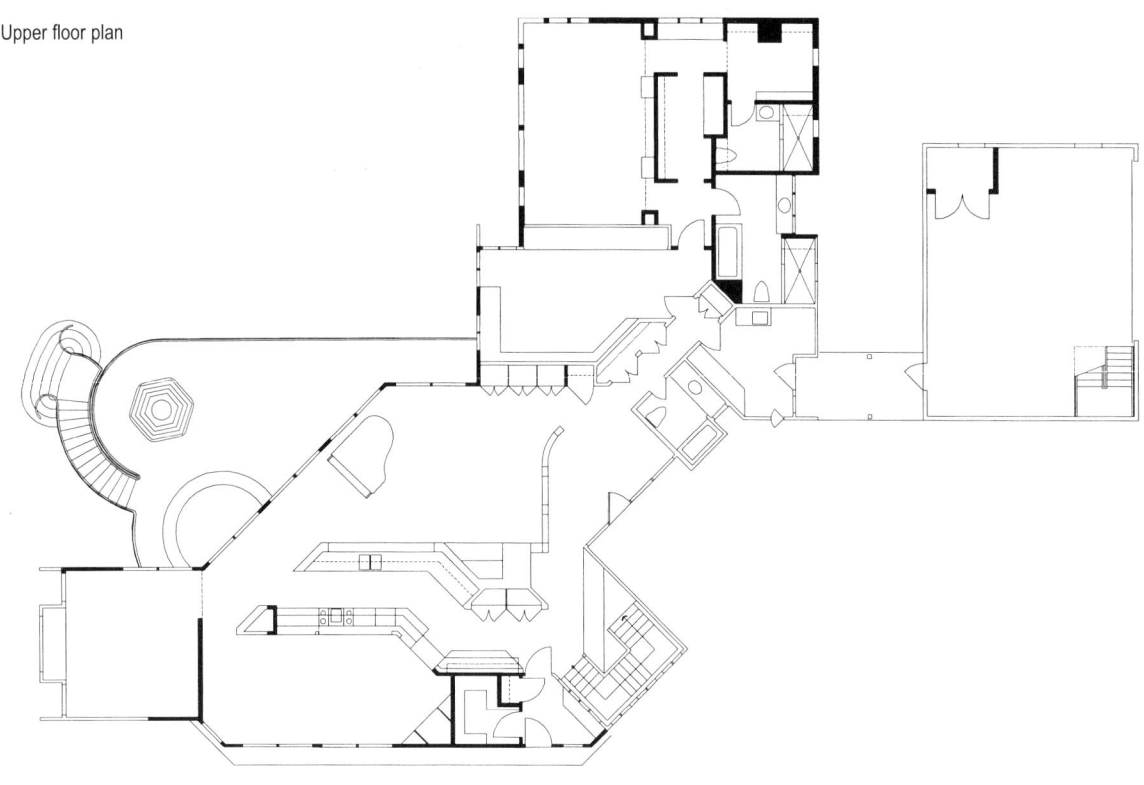

Lower floor plan

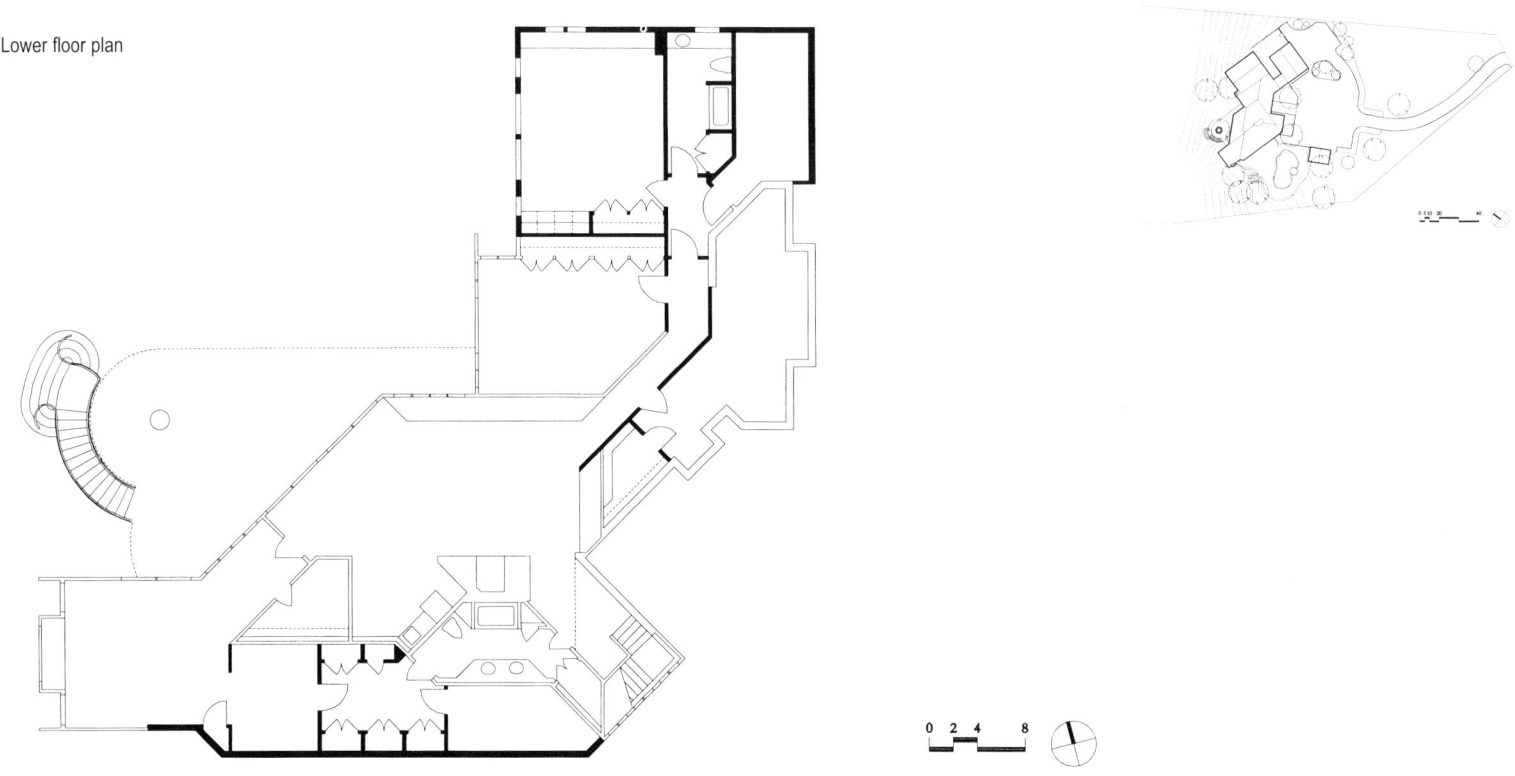

The dining room and the piano corner are developed at the west end of the building, and in both spaces large windows are used to open up the interior towards the garden.
The most outstanding feature of this project is the attempt to integrate the house into its environment. The construction and the landscape melt into harmonious unity. The main factor in this balance is wood, which is found throughout the whole building.
Another important feature is the terrace which gives access to the garden from the first floor. The organic forms of the staircase, which integrates the tree in the overall design, constitute a clear declaration of principles.

83

Dennis Wedlick Architect
Katz House

East Hampton, New York

The clients, Myra and Eli Katz, had been looking for a house for some time but had not found one to their taste. It was then that they decided to buy a site and build the dwelling on it. Dennis Wedlick took charge of the design, which had a very specific basis: the relationship of the house with the environment, not only from an aesthetic but also from a historical point of view. The site is located in Sagaponack, in the state of New York, an area with a long farming tradition. The clients wanted a house that conjugated the traditions and vernacular building structures with the new architectural trends. They thus took the old sheds for storing potatoes that are typical of the region as a model on which to develop the project. The result was a house of 5,000 square feet with six bedrooms, four bathrooms and an enormous living room.

The identifying mark of the dwelling is its roof, or the lack of one. The dwelling is solved as an enormous ogival vault flanked by a series of glazed two-storey lunettes that bring to mind square silos and whose height allows them to be used as interior alcoves.

The dwelling is distributed over two floors and a basement. The ground floor houses the living room, the kitchen, a bedroom with its corresponding bathroom and the garage. On the first floor are the main bedroom, the main bathroom, three other bedrooms, two bathrooms, and a space that the clients have planned to use as a study and a terrace. A door in the main bedroom, now in disuse for reasons of safety (the children are still small) gives onto a balcony overlooking the large, double-height living room. This impressive space is a main feature of the distribution of the interior of the dwelling, with its exposed structure of wooden beams curving upward in an arch. Two elements dominate this room and give it a vague medieval air: a wrought iron chandelier 1.8 meters in diameter that hangs from the ceiling, and an 11-meter high cylindrical chimney that contributes verticality to the space. The entrance door, in the style of the old barns in the area, helps to reinforce the idea of a farm.

◘ Jeff Goldberg / Esto Photographics

Ground floor plan

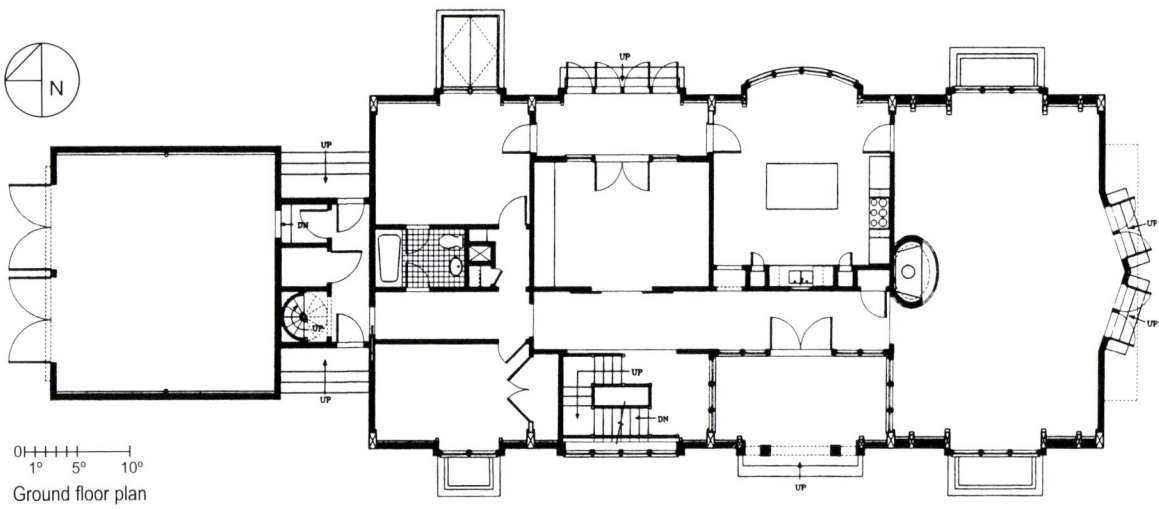

86

South elevation

Due to its imposing height, the dining room invades the first floor. However, the former and the rooms upstairs are only connected by a small balcony in the master bedroom.

First floor plan

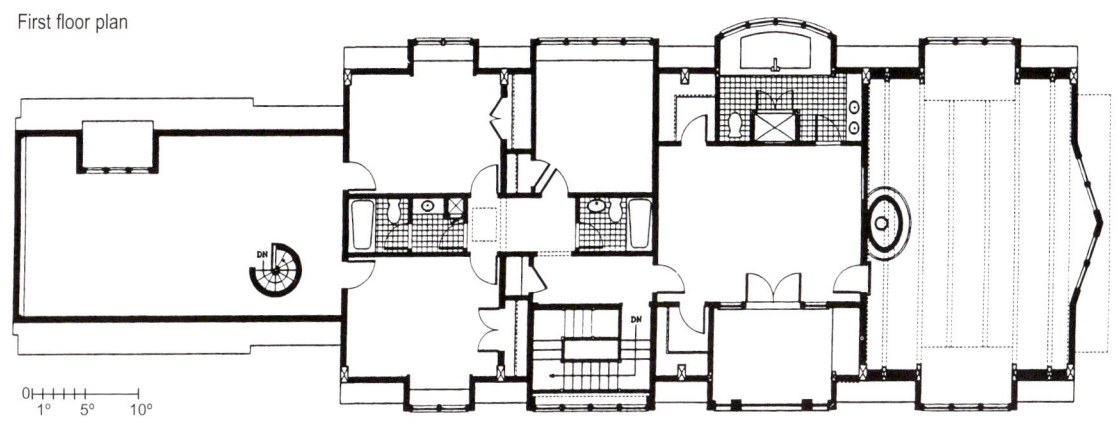

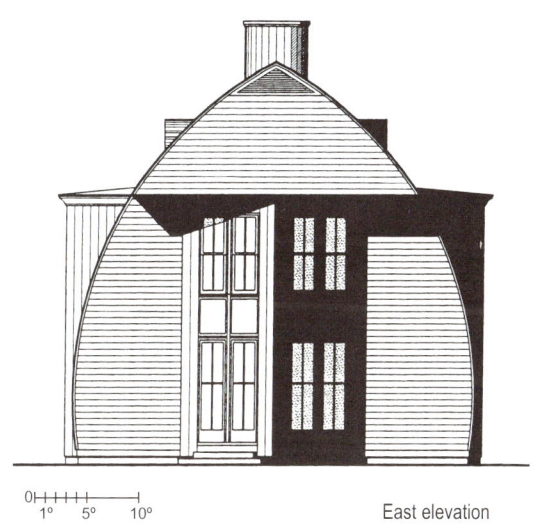

East elevation

South-north section

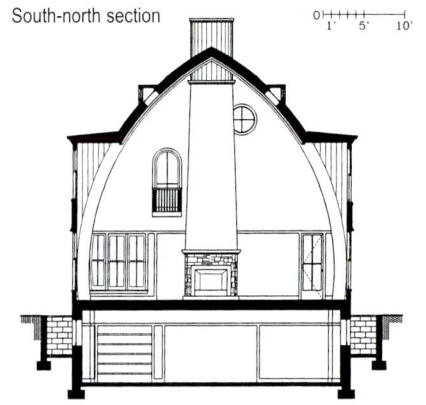

The house has a structure of curved beams, and the side walls clad in cedar wood rise from the foundations to meet in a longitudinal axis. The overall effect is one of balance, with a wooden structure giving a sense of unity to the space.

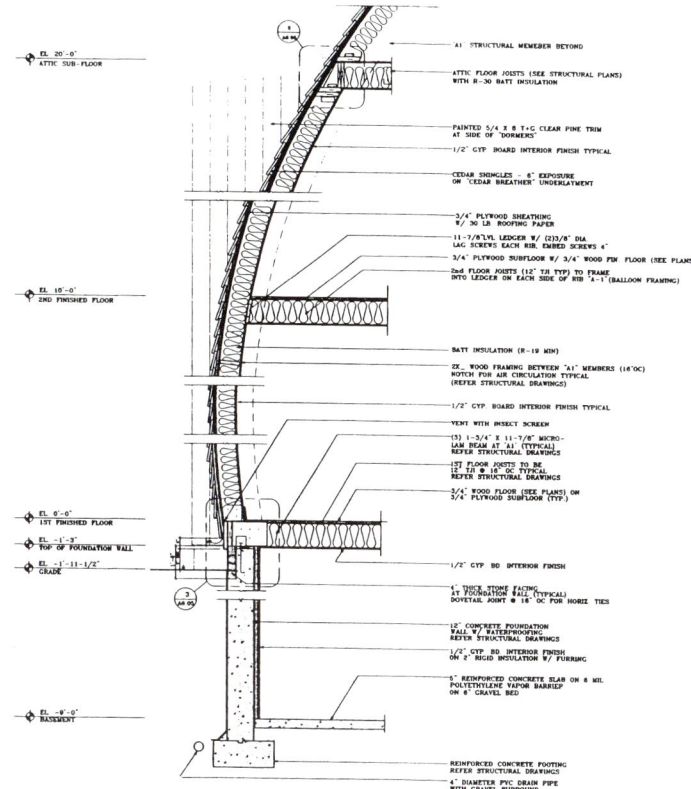

Typical wall section

Entirely clad in wood, the dormers serve a dual purpose: they provide natural light to the interior of the dwelling and act as extensions to the main body. They also give prime ocean views without breaking up the silhouette. Thanks to the glazed dormers, the bedrooms on the second floor visually penetrate the landscape.

Linda Searl, Joseph Valerio
Ohio House
Chicago, Illinois

The streets are the essence of the city. They are a community symbol, a place of encounter. In them lies the tension, even the violence. The urban streets encapsulate everything that we cannot find in the suburbs: light, energy and activity. In a city like Chicago, with such a clear grid plan, the crossroads are critical. It could be said that everything happens at the corners.

Instead of being articulated axially toward each of the streets that converge at a point, the Ohio Street House takes as its axis the same point, the corner, capturing the energy that concentrates at the intersection of the grid.

The design of this dwelling is based on two superimposed forms: a circle and a square that share the same centroid. The dwelling is at the same time open and defensive. On one hand, the construction reflects the discipline of the street; on the other, it receives and absorbs all the unexpected events that happen in it.

Highly expressive materials were used in the construction of the house, underlining the division between the ground floor and the upper floors.

The lower level has a brickwork cladding which does not contrast with the surrounding dwellings. On the upper floors, however, the exterior was clad in grooved metal plates. The facade that gives onto the street seems to be a continuation of that of the ground floor, but the rear part of the dwelling is solved in a different way, in a semicircle.

In the house, the more public elements of the floor plan are developed in parallel to the two streets that form the corner. The living room is aligned with Oakley Street and curves to form the space devoted to the kitchen and dining room, parallel to Ohio Street. Inside this " L " is the staircase. The public spaces are located in the corner giving onto the street, while the private environments are located in the opposite corner. The central staircase leads to the upper levels. The first floor houses the main bedroom, a dressing room and the main bathroom. The second floor houses a bedroom, a bathroom and a large work area.

◻ Barbara Karant/Karant+Associates

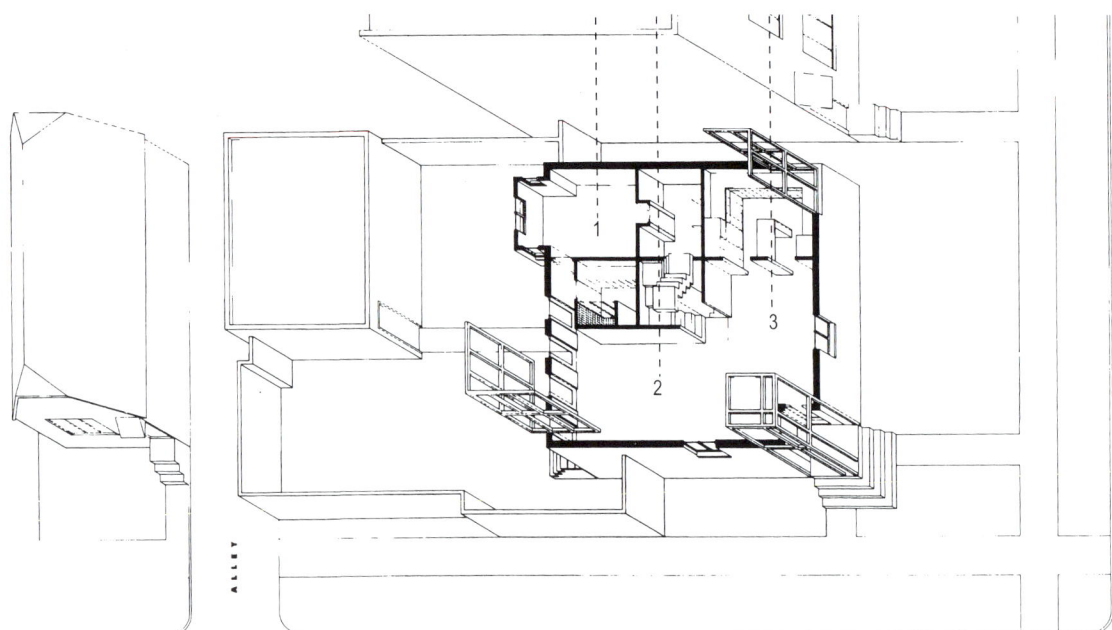

Axonometric view
1. Study
2. Living
3. Dining

The lower level has a square floor plan, while those of the upper levels are semicircular. This difference is also reflected in the materials used for the external lining of each level: white paint on the brick at street level and grooved metal plate on the first and second floors.

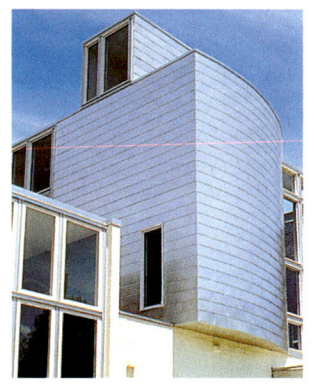

Second floor plan

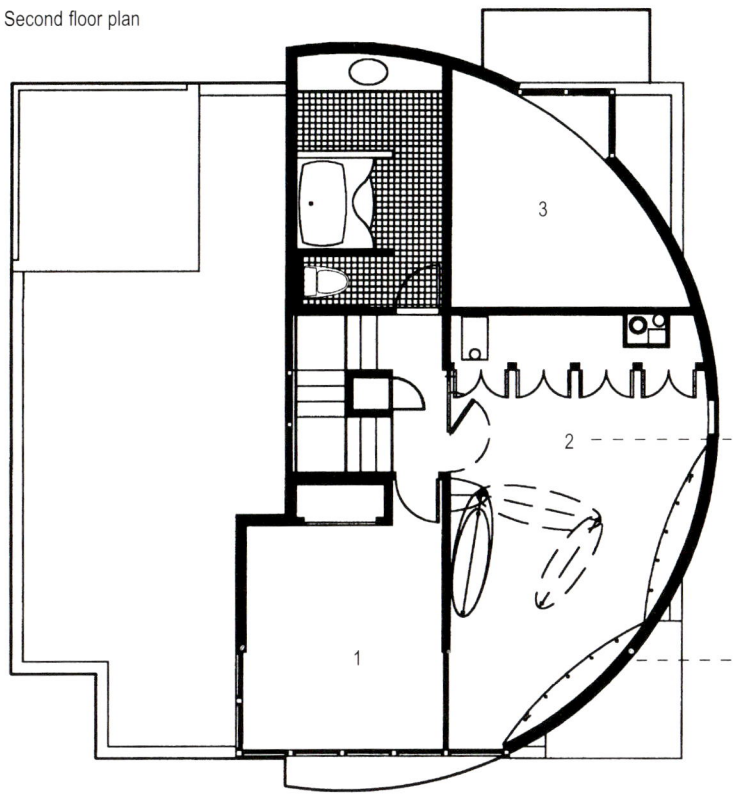

1. Bedroom
2. Workroom
3. Open to below
4. Closet
5. Bedroom

First floor plan

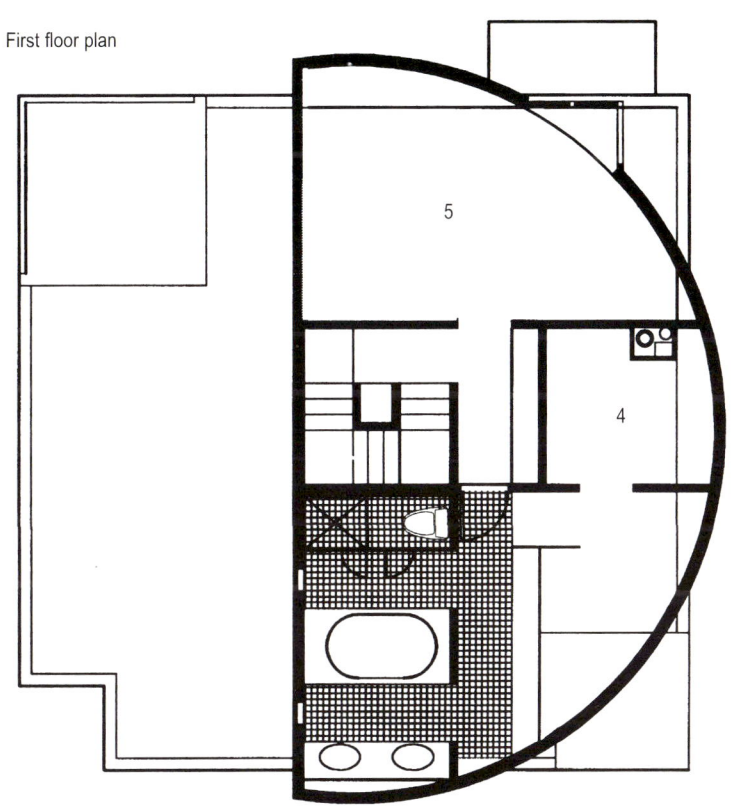

The dwelling was conceived as a polyvalent space, with closely related, almost overlapping atmospheres in an interplay of volumes and heights. Through this spatial and volumetric heterogeneity, the architect is able to diffuse the dividing barriers in the distribution of the interior.

The interplay of volumes on the exterior is reflected inside the dwelling. Wooden panels separate the area of the dining room and the kitchen.

Vincent Ashbahian
Siegal Penthouse
New York City, New York

The main thrust of the design concept was the creation of an open, spacious and airy environment which would allow natural light to filter throughout the interior. To accentuate the natural light, the designers added new window positions and replaced all the existing windows with "Tilt & Turn" units. They opened the living room out to the garden space, building steel and glass French doors and opening a greenhouse to the garden and views of the city. They also built a pergola walkway as a transition to the garden. The main staircase is enclosed in a two-story atrium which is flooded by sunlight. To capitalise on the light, the stairs were designed using a steel and glass construction. 2" thick plate steel was plasma cut into stingers onto which $1/''$ glass treads were mounted. The result is a staircase which sparkles with light. Recessed lighting units were installed to give a similar effect during the evening.

The entrance to the master bathroom is flanked by two steel and glass sliding doors. The glass panes in the door are actually two panes back to back with a sheet of rice paper in between, giving a textured feel to the glass, allowing the light to shine through. The doors were constructed to have no visible trace either on the ceiling or on the floor.

Many amenities have been added to the apartment such as central air conditioning, a heated stone floor in the bathroom, a steam room in the shower area, a Jacuzzi, washer/dryer units, a laundry area and a full office in the bedroom implementing the latest in high-speed phone wiring. The plumbing, air conditioning and electrical systems were completely redesigned.

Peter Aaron/Esto Photographics

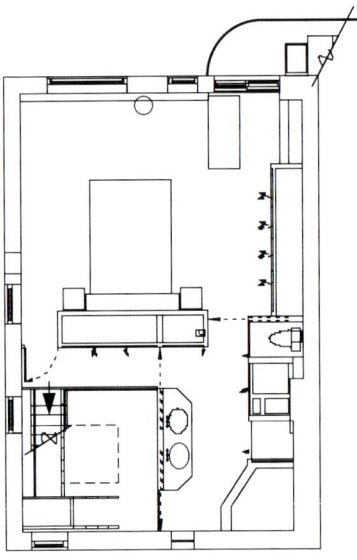

Eigth floor plan

The dining room table was built using ebony maple wood and solid mahogany wood with welded brass legs. The table opens using a custom designed extension system which can accommodate 12 diners.

Seventh floor plan

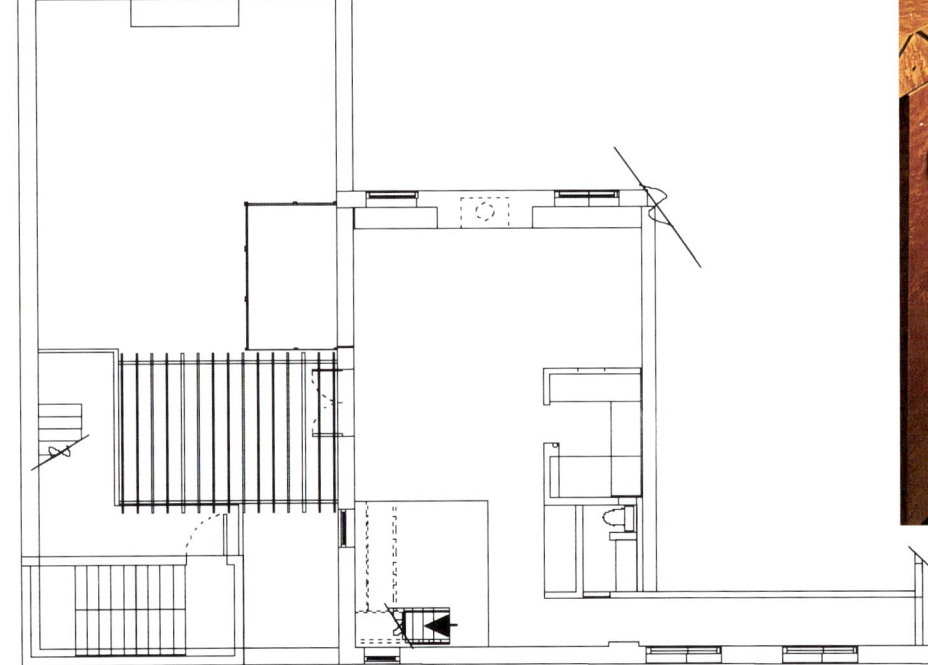

The firm geometry of space and light is achieved thanks to the pure lines of the steel and glass staircase, which contrasts with the wood of the floor and facilitates the use of natural light.

107

The vertical wall against which the bed is placed acts as a partition between bedroom and bathroom. The doors that separate them are made with glass without visible guides, thus creating a visual continuum between the two spaces and accentuating the sensation of width and brightness that served as a guideline for the project.

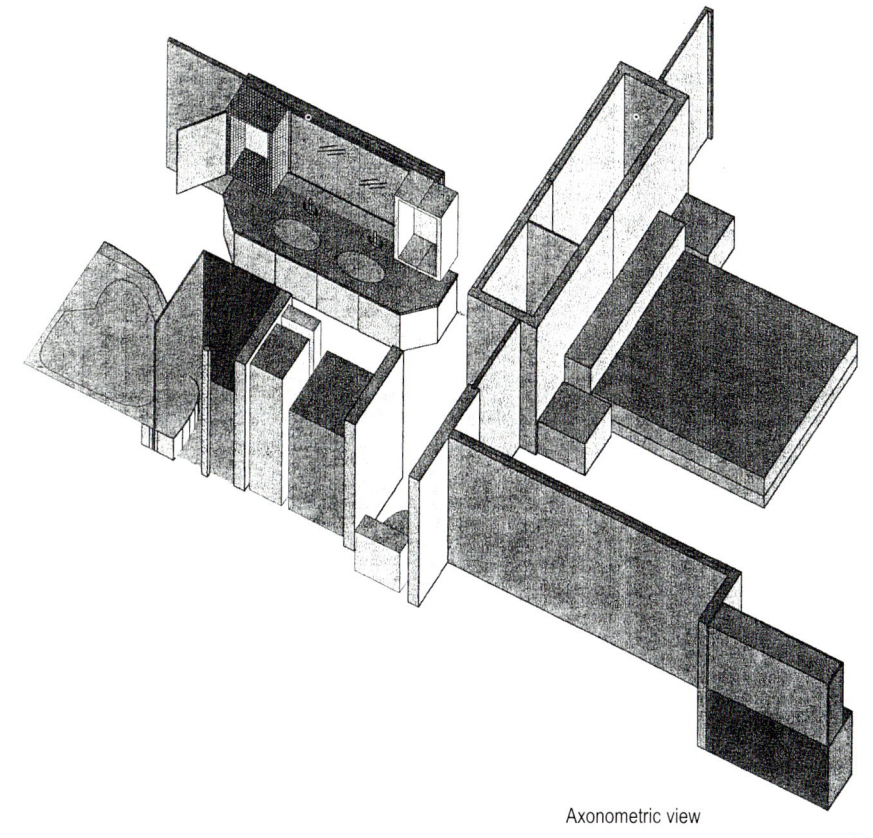

Axonometric view

Moneo Brock Studio
Tribeca Home and Studio
New York City, New York

The space lies on the tenth and top floor of a 1898 warehouse building in Tribeca in New York City. The difficulties presented by the space in its original form were: its low ceiling height, its triangular plan, its tight column grid, and the presence of low-hanging pipes throughout the space. The positive attributes presented by the space were excellent views, exclusive access to the roof, as well as the option to add skylights to provide light, air and a sense of greater openness. The 14" x 14" posts of white oak and 8" x 12" beams of yellow pine were also recognised as assets effusing an air of stout solidity.

In the plan the architects attempted to preserve as much as possible the feeling of open space found in the existing conditions; indeed, by opening the roof in strategic locations, that feeling was accentuated, providing, at the same time, the amenities required for living. Part of the strategy was to keep interventions clear of the columns and leave them on view, allowing the continuity of the structure to remain explicit and to thereby carry a sense of openness and fluidity of space.

The central column line, with its major beam running north-south, naturally divides the space in two. The area to the east of this line was designated as a studio space, and the entry was moved to the west side of the line. The entry path parallel to the column line emphasizes the strength of the structure moving throughout the space, while maximizing the useful area in the studio. Over the studio area existed a large north-facing skylight that gave volume to the space. This was cleaned up and painted a warm yellow.

The area to the west of the column line was designated as living space. An existing roof opening to the south of this area was moved northward to sit directly over a module of the column grid, and a tall skylight with south-facing glass constructed atop. In the south glass of this skylight are operable windows and a door giving access to the roof deck. Furthermore, a folding aluminum stair with a landing made of glass tiles gives access to the high windows and the door. Over the living area, recesses were built into the ceiling, where the spacing of the joists allowed. In these recesses, lights were placed behind planes of diffusing plexiglass to illuminate the room without glare and free from protruding elements below the ceiling surface. Over the entry hall, a similar construction gives a diffuse, general light.

The rooms requiring fixed connexions to the plumbing stack and/or solid enclosure for privacy (the kitchen, the two bathrooms and the bedroom) are constructed in a block to the west of the entry path which was designed to appear as an independent volume, as a large, fixed furniture piece. The block has been kept away from the exterior brick walls and the central column line, and encloses just one column.

◻ Michael Moran

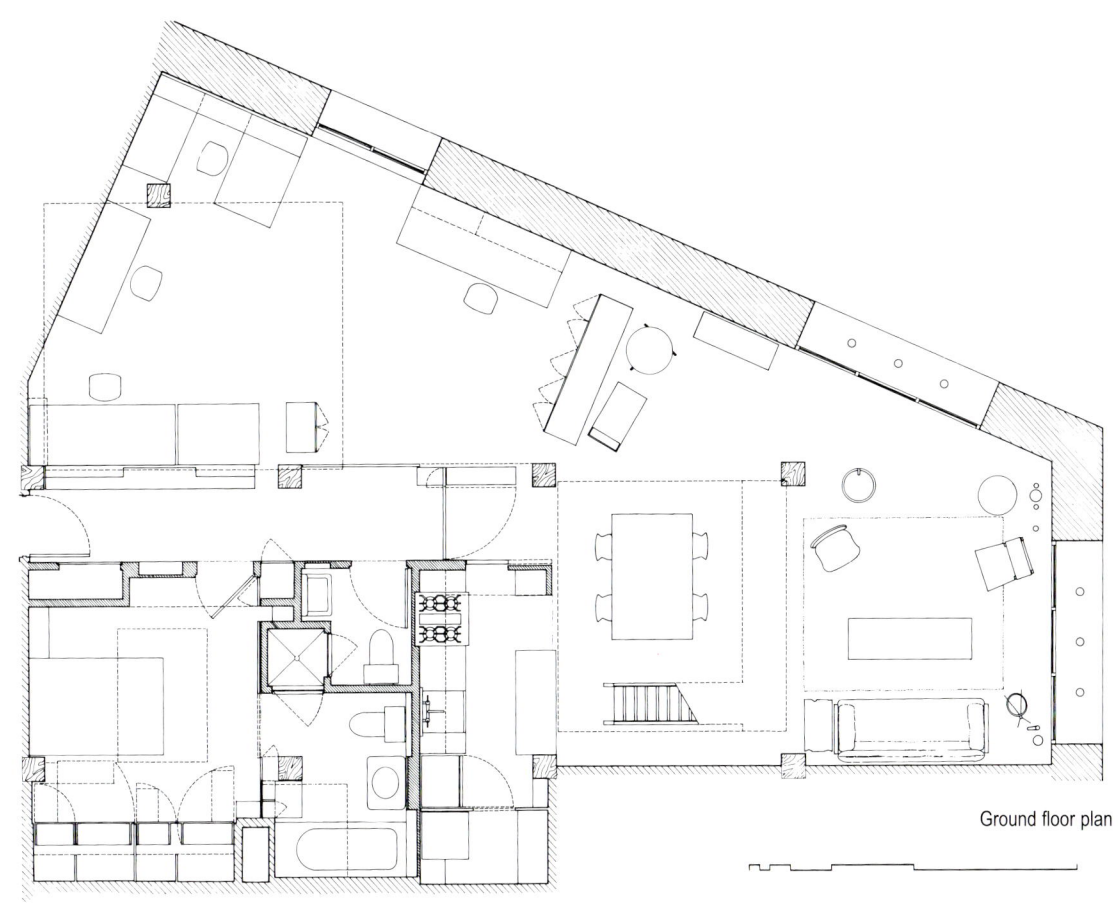

Ground floor plan

The stairway to the roof deck is rigged to a counterweight and can be lifted easily overhead to clear space in the living area. The glass floor is supported by a structure composed of a 6" steel channel as main beam and nine 2" T and two 2" angle sections as subsidiary supports. The steel sections were painted aluminium to match the stair, which is a ship's ladder, a prefabricated product.

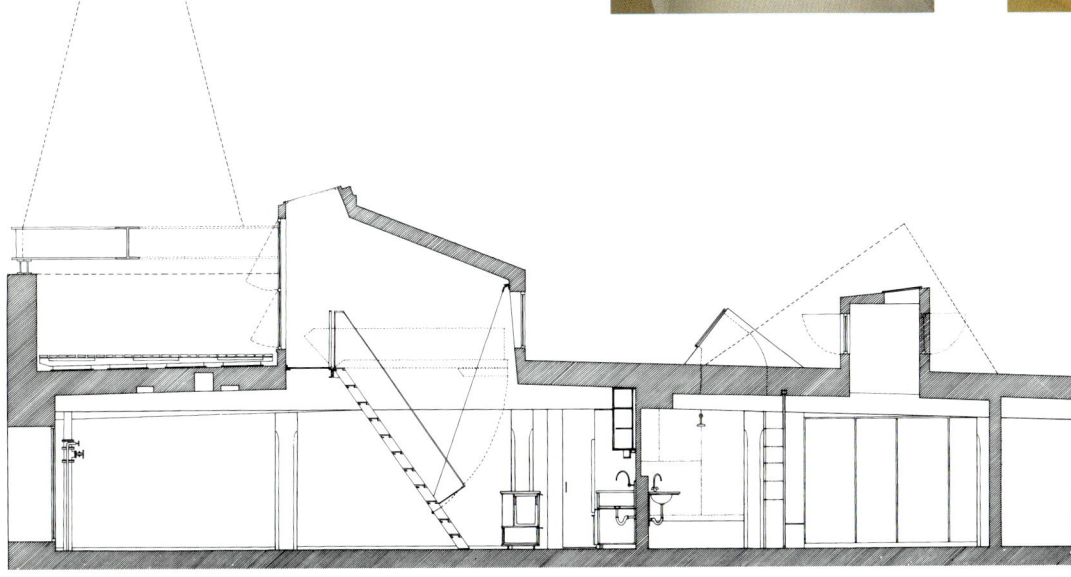

Longitudinal section

113

What most excited the architects about the living area skylight was that one of the building's rooftop water tanks was also brought into view by the placement of the glass wall high above the floor of the loft, giving the vertical dimension extra emphasis.

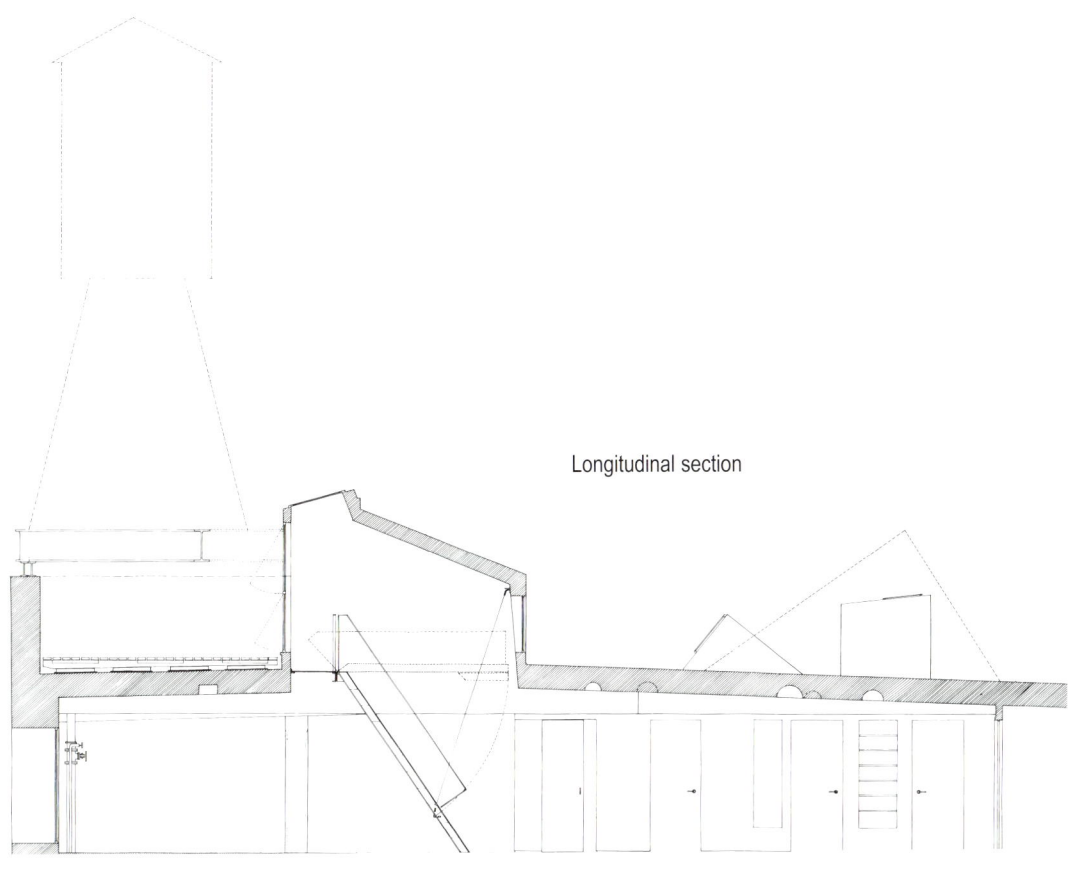

Longitudinal section

Public and private spaces are differentiated both stucturally and visually. The Oriented Strandboard used to clad the walls of the block composed of bedroom, bathrooms and kitchen sharply contrasts with the wooden posts and beams and gives the loft an industrial appearance.

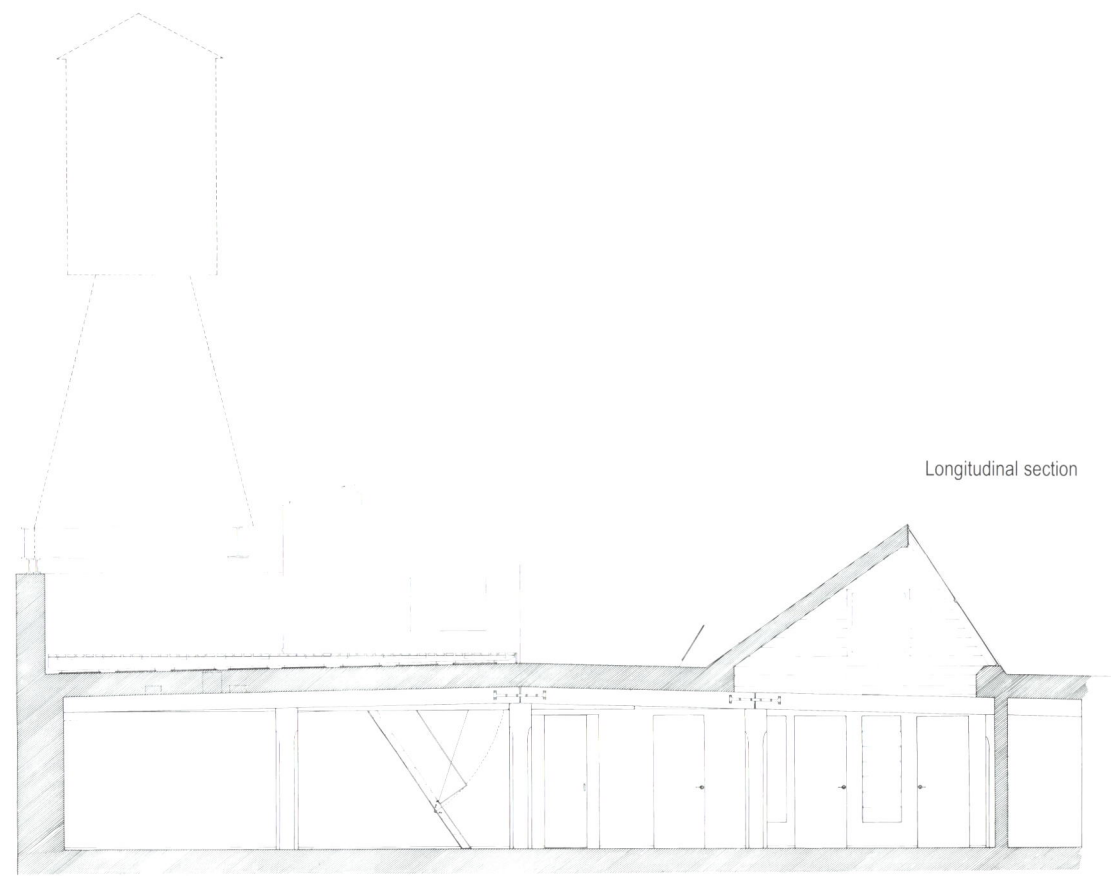

Longitudinal section

Charles Gwathmey, Robert Siegel
San Onofre Residence
Pacific Palisades, California

This residence is located on one and a half acres in a quiet residential neighbourhood near the top of Malibu Canyon. The main living spaces occupy a three-storey curved limestone pavilion that sits on a promontory facing the South and East. Support space fills a three-story cube embedded in the slope behind, overlooking the canyon to the west. Becoming an object in the land, the support building anchors and stabilises the pavilion which, in turn, becomes an object on the land. The curved limestone wall transforms the experience of the landscape as one moves through it from the support building into the explosion of vistas and space revealed by the pavilion's glazed facade.

An autocourt at the entry level leads from the cul-de-sac to an entrance hall that accommodates the vertical circulation. From this point, one passes over a bridge, through the wall of the pavilion, and into the double-height living room. To the West, a window punched into the curve of the pavilion reveals the canyon. The kitchen and the master bedroom above become one and float within the space of the pavilion, forming a boundary between the living and the dining area. The breakfast room penetrates the screen of the glazed facade and creates an outdoor terrace for the bedroom above. At ground level, the entertainment room recessed within the curve of the pavilion creates a shaded terrace that opens onto the southern lawn and leads back to the swimming pool and spa facing the canyon. The support building is organised bilaterally. In the perimeter looking out over Malibu Canyon are the excercise room on the lower level, the guest bedrooms on the entry level, and an office/conference area on the upper level. In the core, a screening room and archival storage area occupy the lower level; storage and service areas are behind the garage on entry level. On the upper level, the master dressing room and bath opposite the office are rotated on axis with the bridge leading back to the pavilion.

◘ Farshid Assassi/Assassi Productions

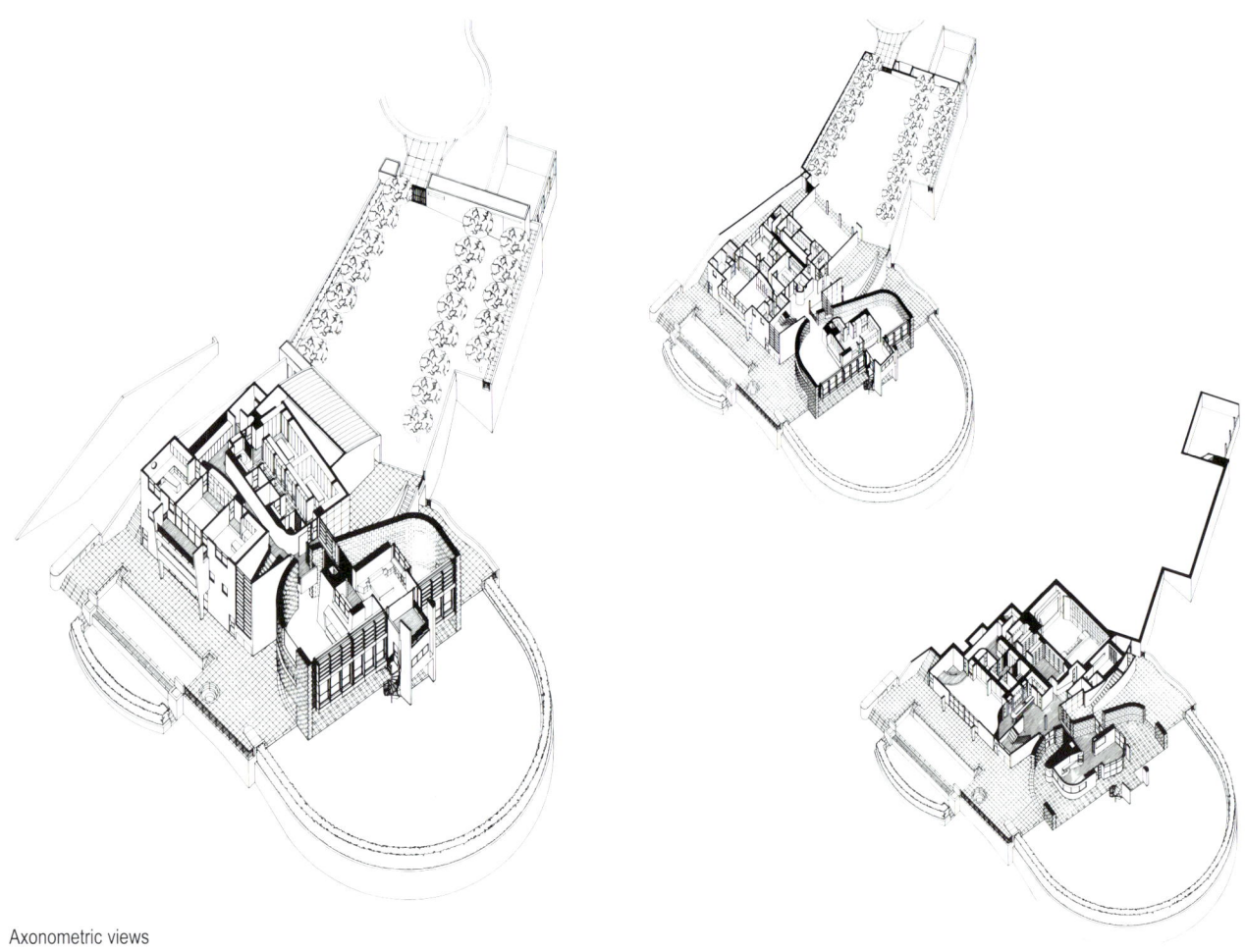

Axonometric views

The stainless steel wall panels articulating the facade of the stuccoed support building and the stainless steel brise-soleil contrasting with the curved limestone wall of the pavilion all help to visually reinforce the collage of the materials employed in the building.

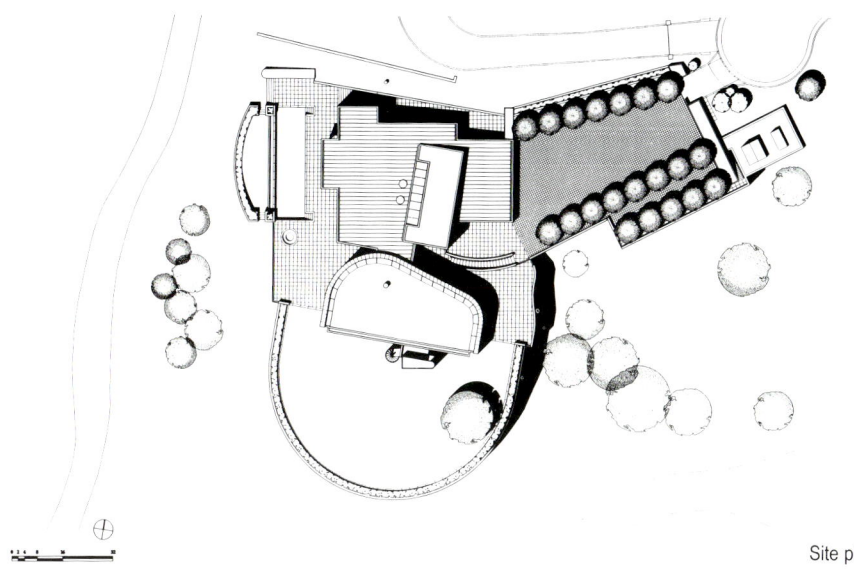

Site plan

123

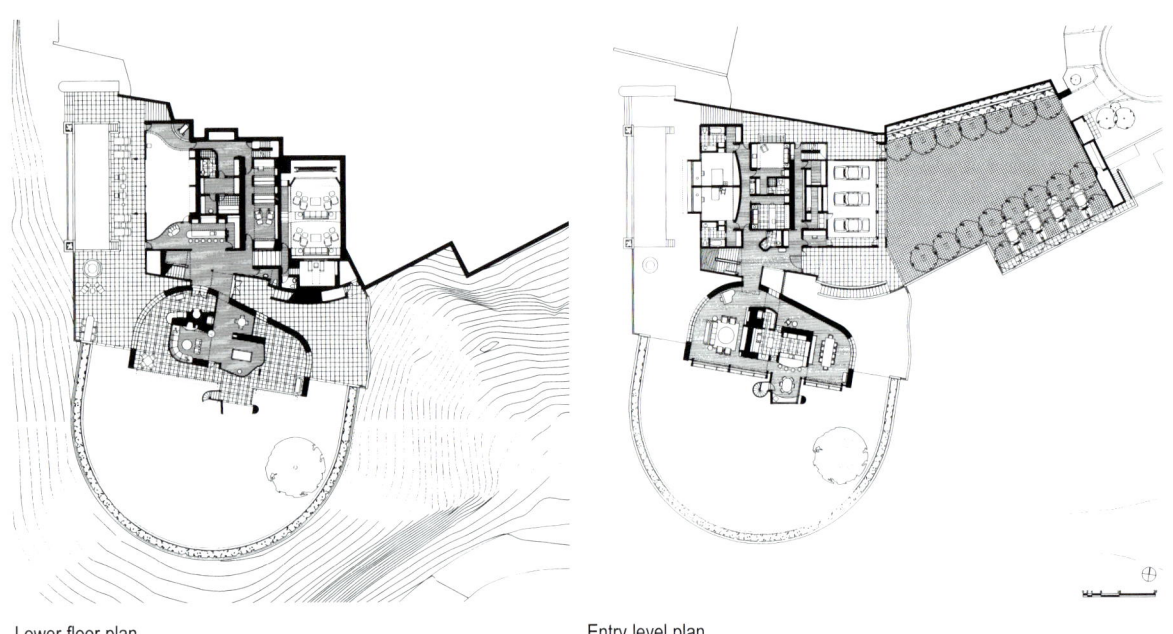

Lower floor plan

Entry level plan

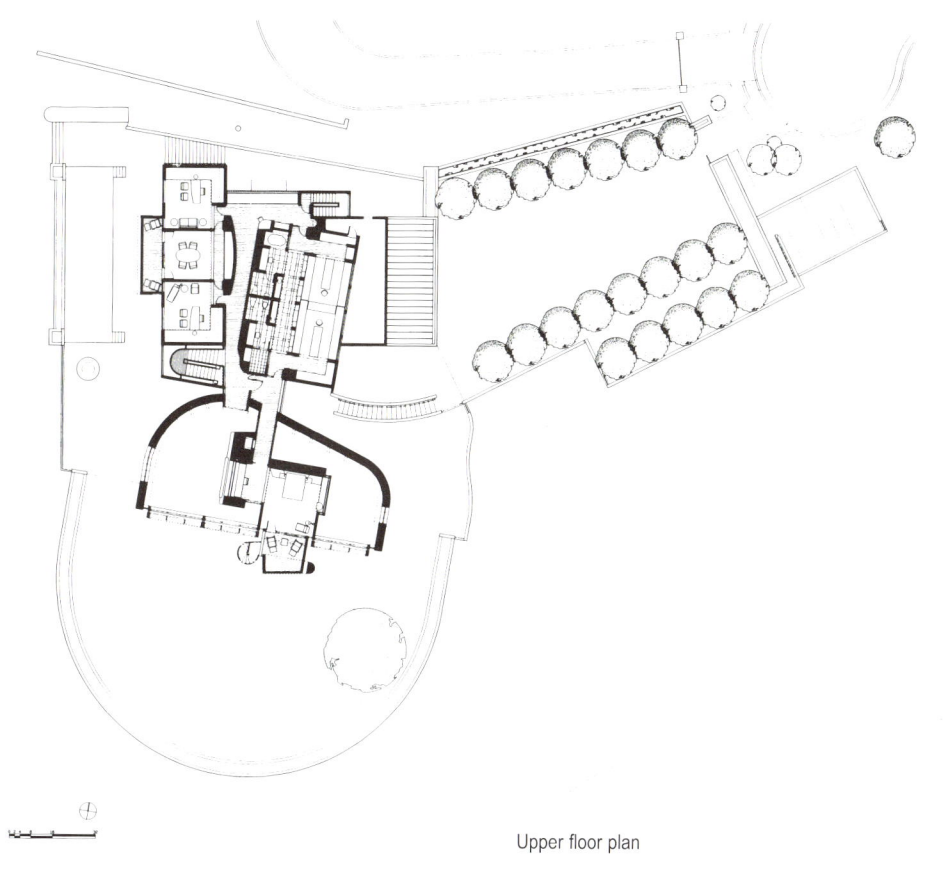

Upper floor plan

Cheng Design
Hogan/Mayo Residence
Rancho Santa Fe, California

At the time of its acquisition, the site on which this dwelling stands was occupied by an old ranch. The clients decided to demolish it and build a new house combining clarity and warmth.

A long rectangular ground plan similar to that of the original construction was chosen. The main entrance, the private entrance, the ground floor rooms and the main bedroom converge in an interior-exterior space that acts as a sheltered area and a pergola. The two entrances seek to produce the sensation of transit: a stone walkway forms the private rear entrance, while the main entrance is formed by a staircase similar to that of a ship, with steel cable handrails.

The construction is clad in corrugated metal sheet, which was also used on the roof to optimise rainwater drainage. The discreet presence of wooden strips and boarding on the exterior evokes the vernacular constructions of the area. The walls of the main bedroom, the ground floor corridor and the kitchen were built with reinforced concrete cast in situ.

The walkway of the rear entrance ends in a concrete block stamped with symbols from the I Ching. The two hexagrams on the wall represent the concepts "reduction" and "limitation", interpretations taken from the divinatory methods of The Book of Changes. As in all Cheng Design projects, the clients, the manufacturer, the site foreman and Fu-Tu Cheng, director of the Cheng design study, threw their coins into the air just before laying the foundations of the house in order to establish a connection with the spirit of change and non-permanence and to obtain spiritual guidance for the participants in the project. In the house we can also find other symbols that represent "water", "infinity" and "work", as well as several objects that were recovered from the site or —like the doorknob— found in the local flea-market.

◘ Debbie Beacham

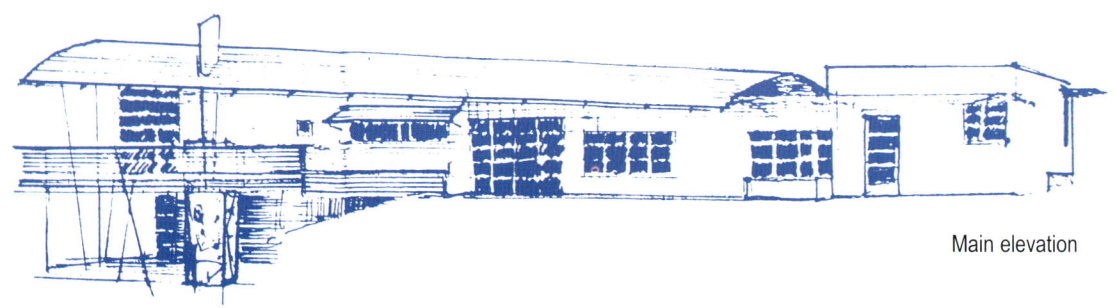

Main elevation

The house's exterior cladding combines wood, glass and corrugated metal. The latter is shown here to be a highly versatile material, which combines a light look with structural durability.

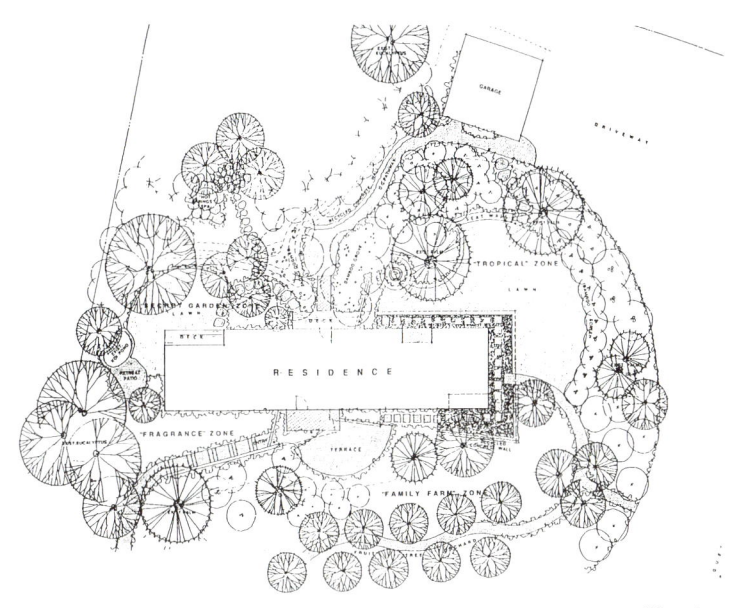

Site plan

Sketches

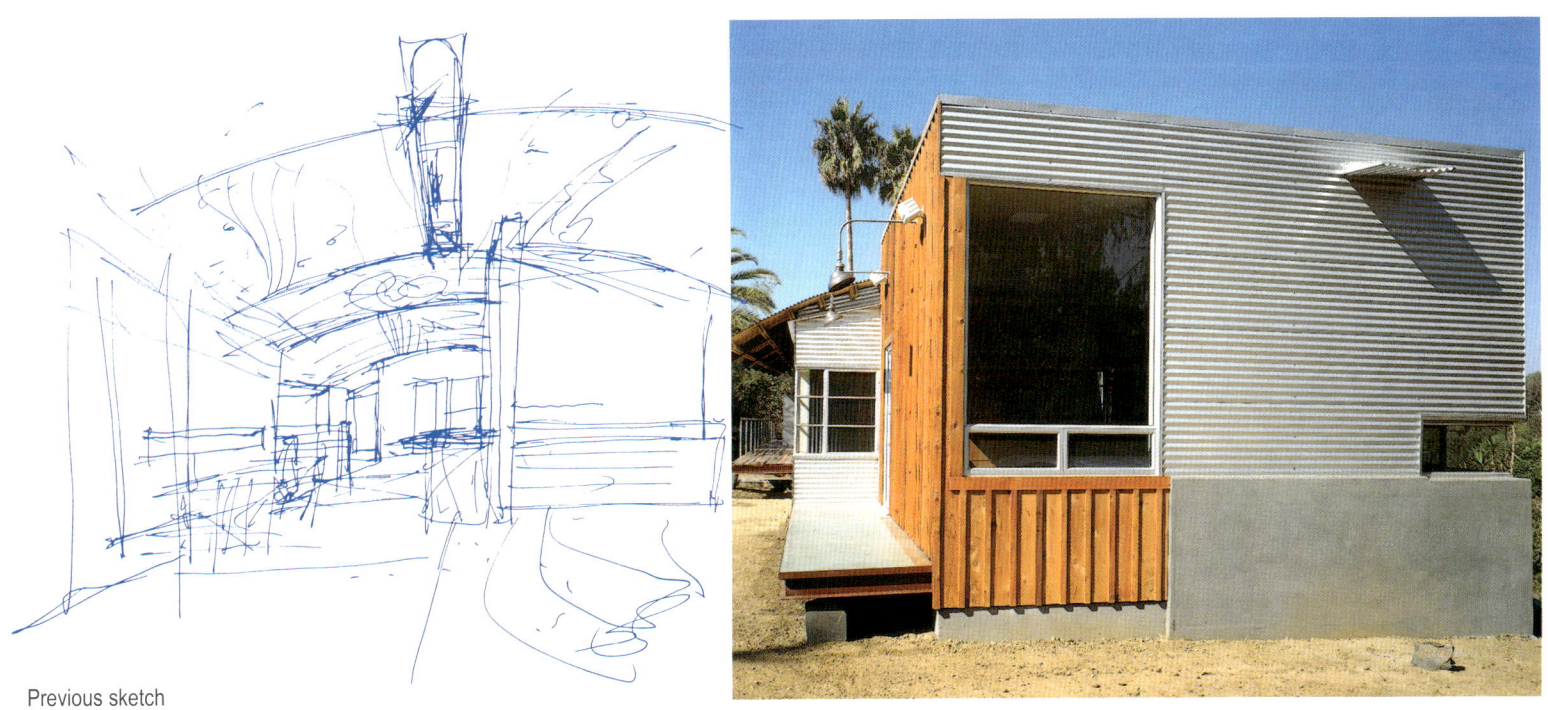

Previous sketch

134

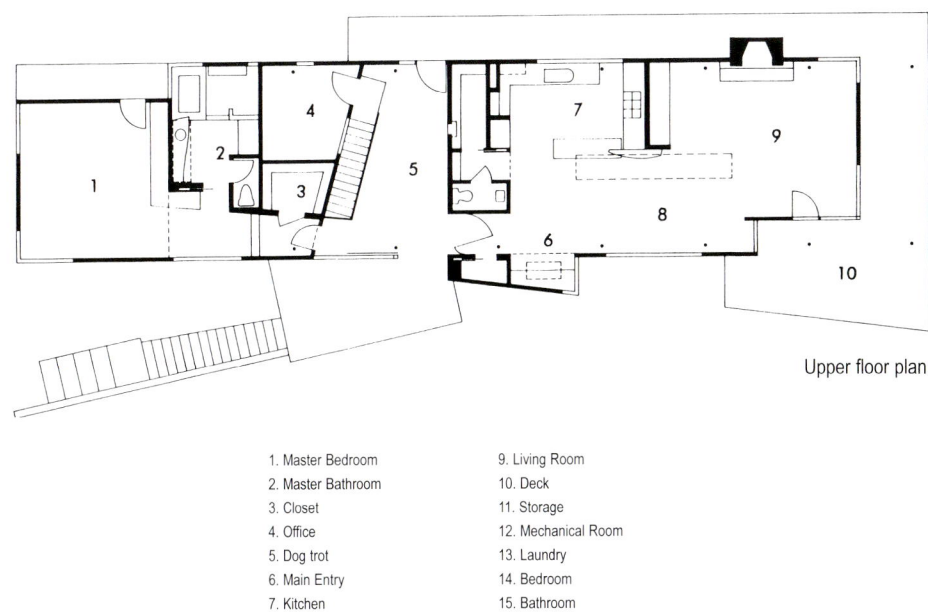

Upper floor plan

1. Master Bedroom
2. Master Bathroom
3. Closet
4. Office
5. Dog trot
6. Main Entry
7. Kitchen
8. Dining Room
9. Living Room
10. Deck
11. Storage
12. Mechanical Room
13. Laundry
14. Bedroom
15. Bathroom
16. Library

Large picture windows maximise the light and longitudinal spaces running the length of the corridor usher in zenital light. The exterior of the home is reflected in the interior with steel and wire handrails and juxtapositions of levels and bare structures.

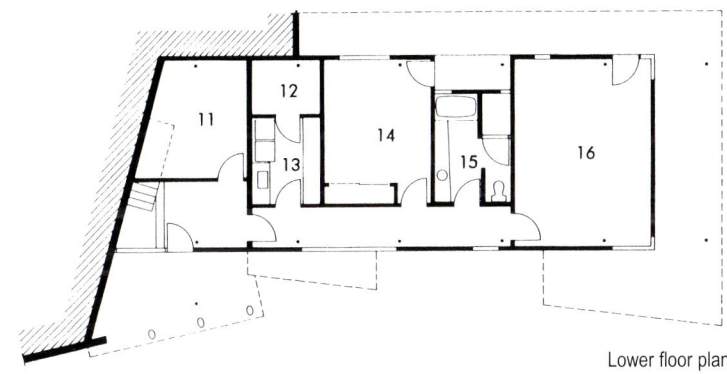

Lower floor plan

Hariri & Hariri Architects
Riverbend House
Great Falls, Virginia

A house without a client, this 5,000 Square Feet house was built on speculation by a developer in Great Falls, Virginia, serving as a testing ground for home buyers preparing for the housing innovations of the twenty-first century. It attempts to redefine the lifestyle of the "single family unit", challenging standard expectations of suburban homes and including concepts of resale value, superficiality of appearance, and the American Dream.

In contrast to the opulent façade with enormous porticoes supported by vinyl Corinthian columns of the traditional American house, the entry to this house provides an intermedial transit space between the interior and the exterior. The entrance slips between two walls, creating a well-marked but simple introduction to the house. The site is a heavily wooded landscape, sloping sharply down to a creek. The water, moving through the site, becomes a major element, creating a contemplative sound, a reminder of the passage of time within the stillness of the setting.

The house is divided into two parts, spatially, formally, programmatically and structurally. One part is earthbound with heavy masonry structuring that follows the contour and curvature of the land. This curved volume creates an entry court and houses the private spaces of the house (bedrooms, kitchen and the guest suite). The other part is sky bound with a light, wing-like structure that floats above the earth. It is supported by steel columns and is mostly enclosed by glass curtain walls. This part of the house contains all the public areas (family room, dining room and living room) and is roofed with a precisely formed folded plane; lifting upwards as it stretches over the house, it emphasises the human desire for weightlessness. At its base, the house contains a large open terrace. This area is well integrated into the house and the existing landscape, and replaces the typical "front and back lawn" of suburban living.

◻ Jeff Goldberg/Esto Photographics

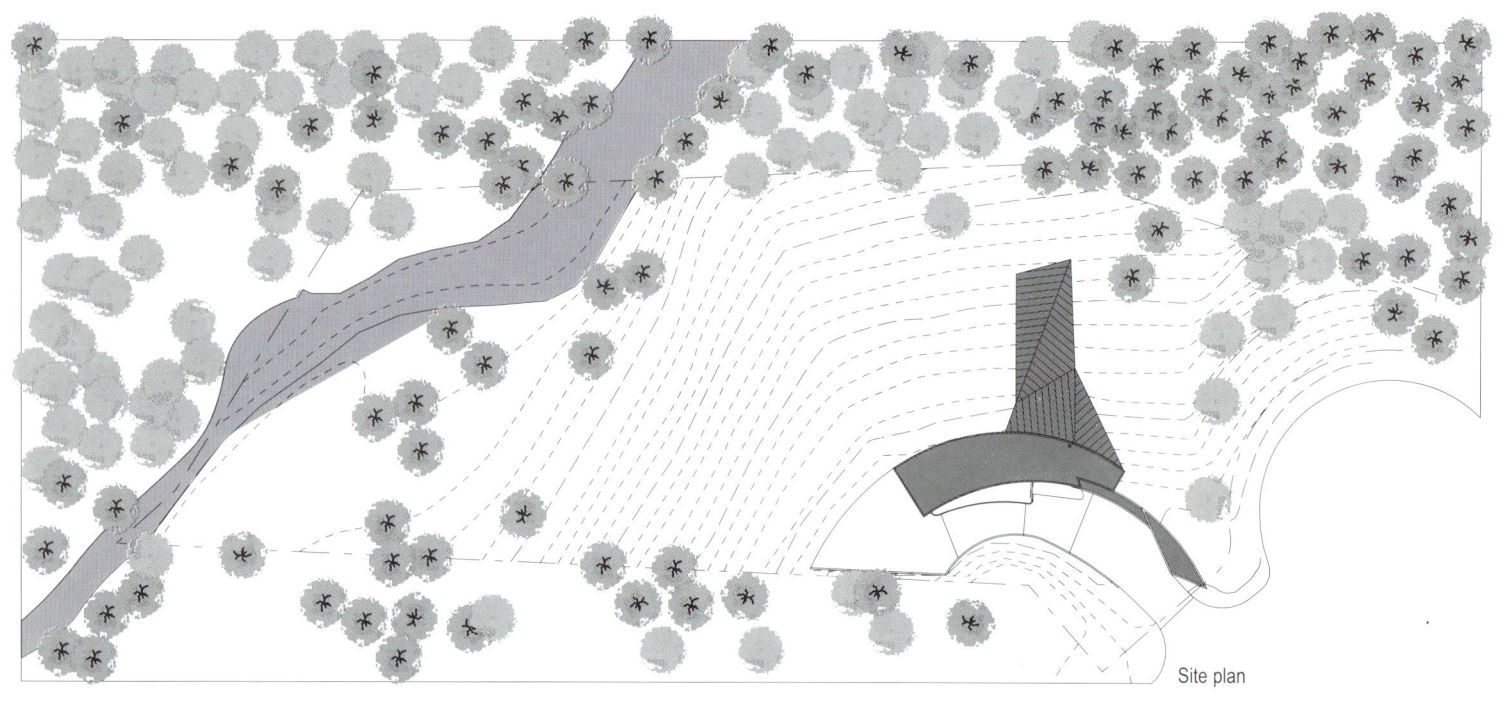

Site plan

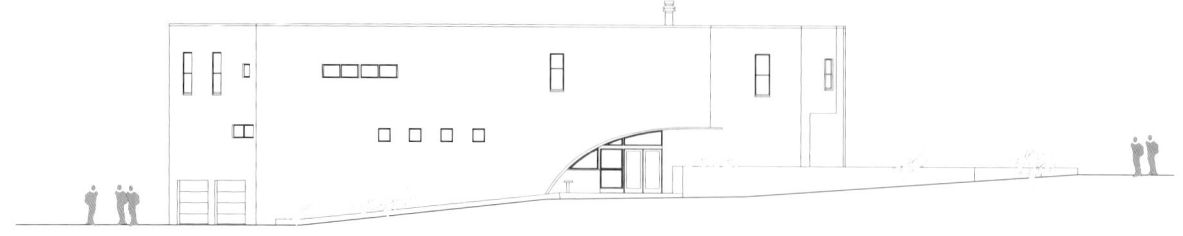

South elevation

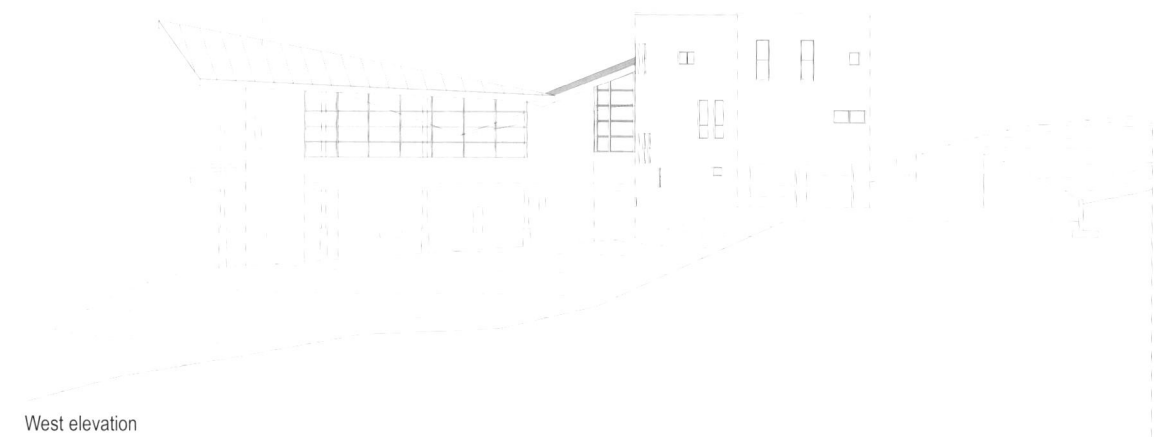

West elevation

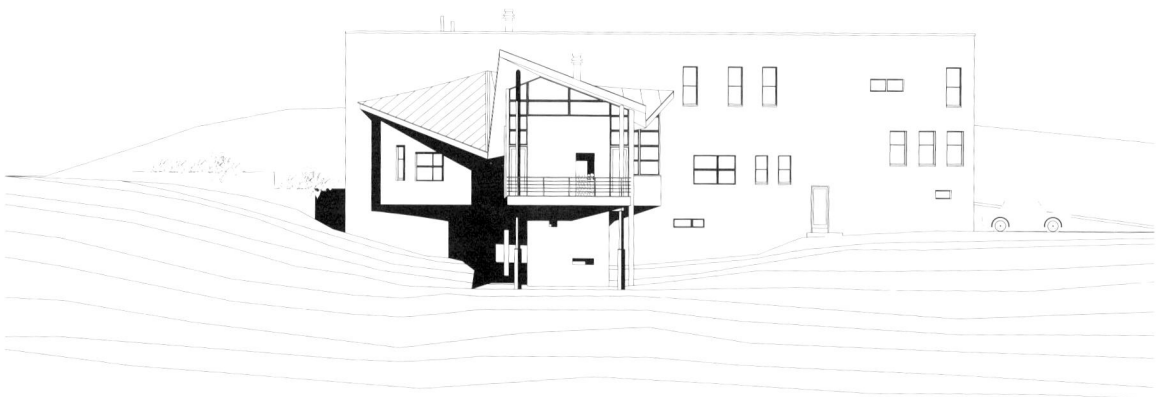

North elevation

East elevation

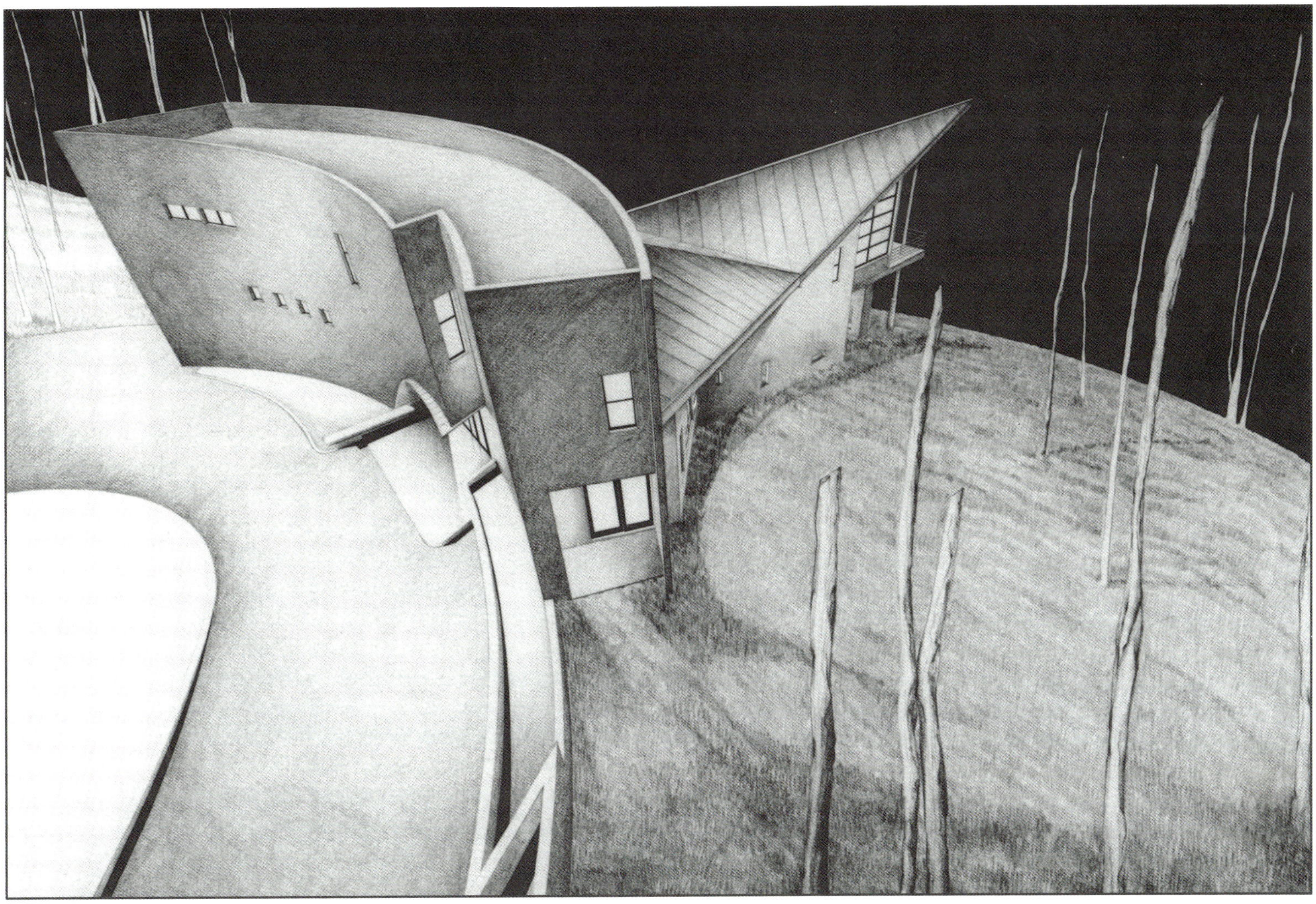

141

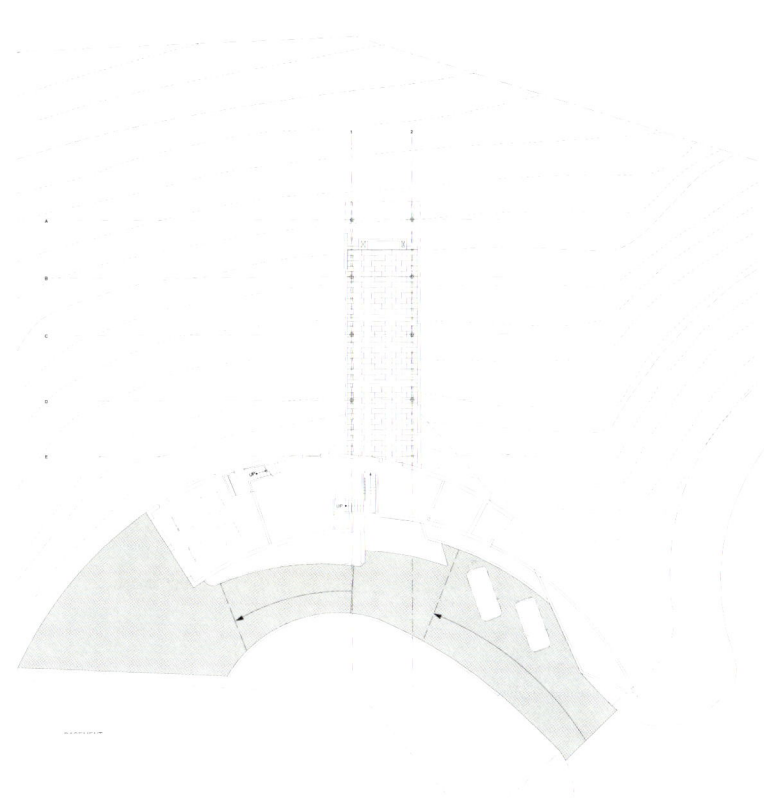
Basement floor plan

First floor plan

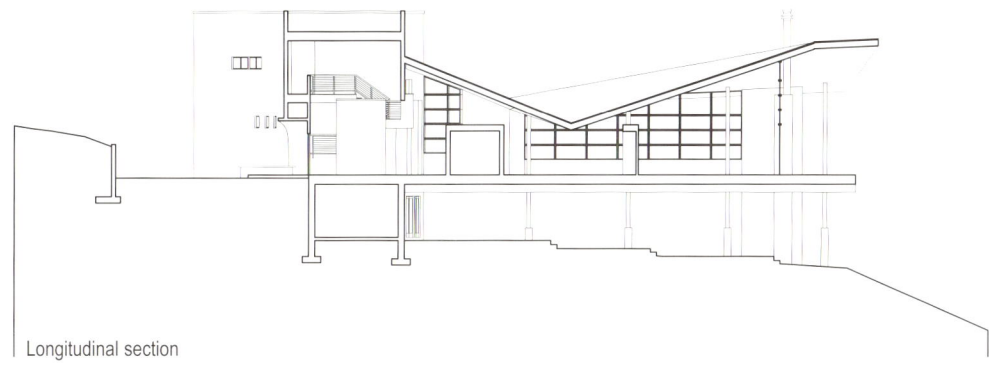

Longitudinal section

A curved structure houses the private spaces of the residence. The topography of the site, with its sharp slope, favors a peculiar layout of the windows in the bathroom and kitchen. The top lighting of these spaces creates a feeling of intimacy and privacy.

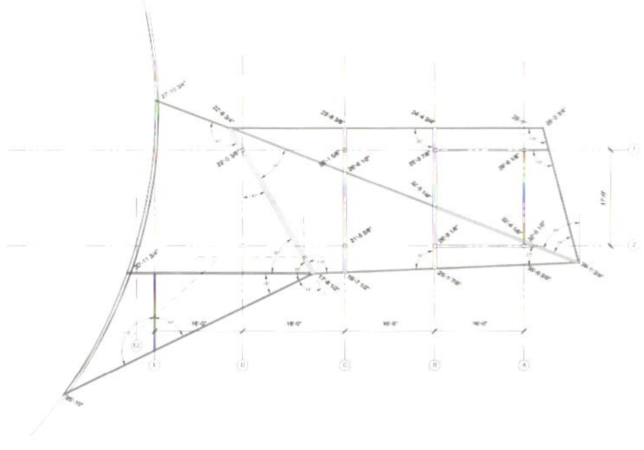

Diagram of the steel roofing stucture

Hanrahan & Meyers
Kern Apartment/Moma Tower

New York City, New York

This project is a renovation of a 1500 square foot apartment in the Museum of Modern Art Tower in New York City. The relatively small size of the apartment required the development of an intricate set of details and innovations in spatial planning in order to create a sense of expanse and dimension. As a complement to this idea and the small but extraordinary art collection that includes Cy Twombly, Henry Moore, Francis Bacon and Toulouse-Lautrec, the space was composed with intense colours and materials to give a visual and tactile richness to the apartment.

All of the walls in the apartment are finished with white plaster. The exterior coating of the apartment is matt white plaster. The wall separating the living room and the boudoir is polished white plaster and contains a movable translucent glass plane. The combination of matt and reflective surfaces within the apartment establishes an effect of movement through the interaction between active and inactive surfaces.

A single seven-foot high cabinet with a piece of curved glass above divides the entrance from the bedroom. The living room has a large cherry cabinet that incorporates a television, stereo, bar and storage space. The living room is defined by a 3-inch thick plaster wall with pivoting steel and glass panel at one end that allows a visual connection between this room and the bedroom.

All of the furniture was selected or designed by the architects.It includes a custom-designed bed of stainless steel, wood and leather and a table of cherry and cold-rolled steel. Isamu Noguchi designed the dining table, are by Le Corbusier and Eileen Gray an other designs pieces.The space was designed using computer technology, through a series of rendered studies. The digital environment allowed the architects to view the space in movement. There is a link between the medium of the sketches (computer animation) and the spatial qualities of the final design.

Jeff Goldberg/Esto Photographics

Reflective and matt surfaces establish a dialogue between active and inactive spaces. The reflective surface of the active plane which bisects the apartment, the movable glass inset within this plane, and the similarly framed mirror at the entrance opposite, all contribute to the interaction of movement between these reflective surfaces and the matt coating of the exterior.

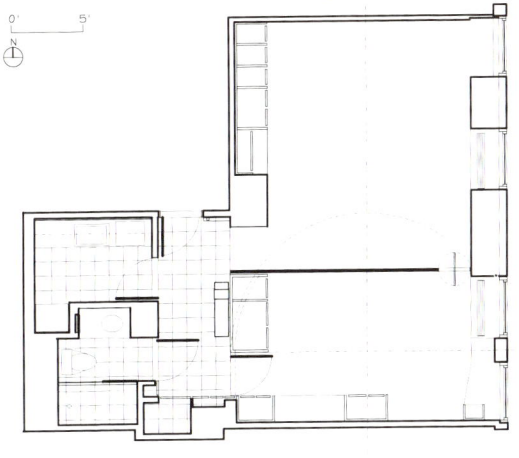

Apartment floor plan

Perspective of the living room, bedroom and access area.

The basic elements of the apartment are wood cabinets and panels. The cabinets are made of hand-rubbed cherry and birch and are positioned at the perimeter of the apartment to open up the space.

Perspective of the main spaces of the dwellings

The entrance is distinguished by a limestone floor with a steel finish, incorporating a small container at the door for keys and other belongings.

153

Joel Sanders Architect
Apartment on Central Park West

New York City, New York

This project, a reconfiguration of a 3,000-square foot apartment in Central Park West in Manhattan, attempts to take maximum advantage of its spectacular panoramic views of the neighbouring Olmsted's Park.

While the design respects the integrity of the original pre-war structure —moldings were repaired and a new parquet floor was installed— the design scheme converts its pre-existing rabbit warren of isolated rooms into an open floor plan that corresponds to the lifestyle and the needs of the clients, a professional couple with young children.

A free-standing mahogany storage wall, replacing a wall of closets that previously blocked the Park view, now separates the living and dining rooms. Sanders introduced a new vocabualary of movable elements —flexible mahogany panelling and pivoting custom-designed aluminium and glass doors— that enables the clients to modify the relation between the apartment's overlapping sequence of domestic spaces.

Besides defining changing levels of privacy, these operable elements frame exterior views. An aluminium railing travels throughout the apartment, changing function as it moves from space to space. Providing support for a glass shelf in the entrance hall, the rail acts as a set of handles for the pivoting dining room partitions before forming the frame for a bookshelf-writing table in the living room alcove.

◘ Peter Aaron/Esto Photographics

Three large pivoting doors of aluminium and glass provide a high level of physical and visual permeability as well as defining different degrees of permeability between rooms.

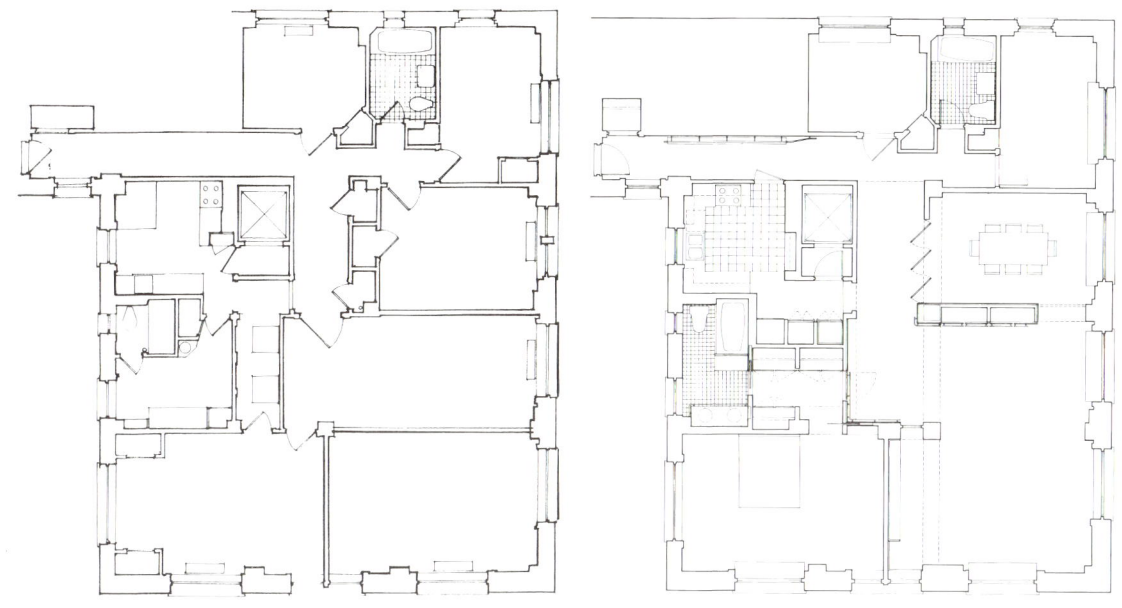

Floor plan before the reconfiguration

Floor plan after the reconfiguration

The restoration project managed to conserve the original character of the dwelling, transforming it into a continuous space that opens onto the magnificent views of Olmsted's Park.

A tubular aluminium profile with a constant section acts as a common reference between the different rooms. It is used in different places as a support for shelves, a towel rail and handles for the pivoting doors.

Roger Hirsch, Susan Frostén, Drew Souza
Fire Island House
Fire Island, New York

This summer house was designed with the intent of creating a space which connected and integrated the interior and exterior spaces, and allowed for an open, flowing space full of natural light and cross breezes.

It was to be a house that created, both visually and physically, a strong connection from the main living spaces out to the pool, decks and trees beyond. This feeling of expansive space and light had to be created within the confines of the program; to efficiently fit four bedrooms and three bathrooms within a compact 1,600 square feet.

The 100-foot long orange wall marks the offset entry to the site, which separates the entry walk from the pool area. The split-level deck gives the orange wall a commanding height of 8 feet along the narrow entry walk, but a less imposing 6 feet on the pool side. At the end of the access walk, a series of steps lead up to the entry level deck. The lower pool deck is separated from the main deck by a linear slot filled with 6' tall grass.

On the first floor, the living room is double height, with exposed wood beams rising to approximately 20 feet. Within this double-height space, the "cube", with its front wall pulled back from the glass façade and its top pulled down from the 20' ceiling above, appears to float over the dining area, supported solely by its open floor joints which extend to meet the front façade. Below this cube, and in contrast to the towering living room space, the dining room has an intimate ceiling height of only 7' 3".

The kitchen, situated behind the dining room, has open shelves of maple and blackened steel with countertops of flat-sheet stainless steel laminated to maple. A taut theatrical fabric scrim separates the kitchen from the dining room. Depending on the ratio of light levels, it either conceals the kitchen almost entirely, or allows for silhouettes of people and objects within. The first floor also includes a guest room and a bathroom within the base of the tall "tower".

The open riser stairs lead to three bedrooms and two bathrooms on the second floor. The master bedroom is within the "tower", with a large pivoting panel overlooking the living room below, the pool outside and glimpses of the bay beyond. The "cube" bedroom has three small, hinged panel openings set back from the glass of the front façade and offering small, framed views of trees, sky and water. On separate sides of the house, each of the upstairs bedrooms has a private balcony which projects out into the tops of the trees. The two upstairs bathrooms are connected by an oversized shower with large acid-etched, pivoting doors and a large operable skylight above.

The design approach and fabrication of the house reflect the constraints of the site and the challenging conditions. There are no paved roads and only service vehicles are allowed access through a central path. All construction materials, cabinetry and furnishings were shipped by ferry and transported on golf cart-sized vehicles via narrow wooden boardwalks.

Many interior fixtures and furnishings —mostly custom-designed for the project— were designed to be shipped in a disassembled, compact form and then reassembled on site. The house itself was constructed on a platform supported by wooden piles driven deep into the soft soil of the sandbar.

☐ Michael Moran

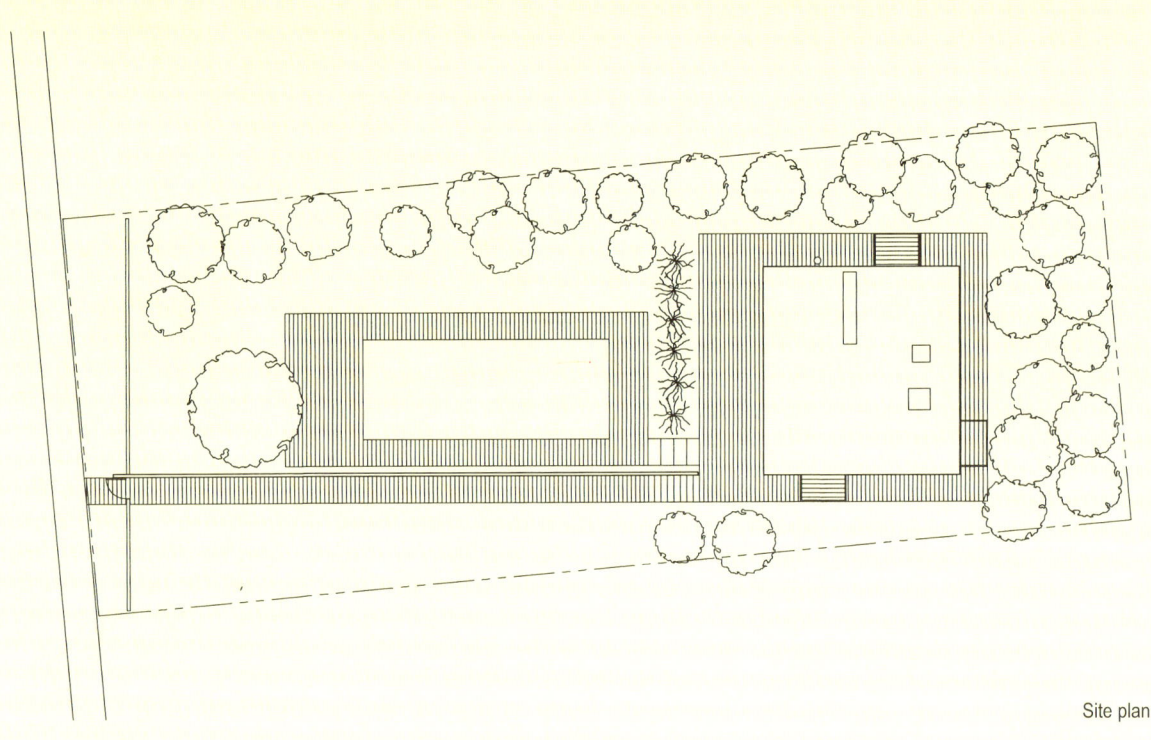

Site plan

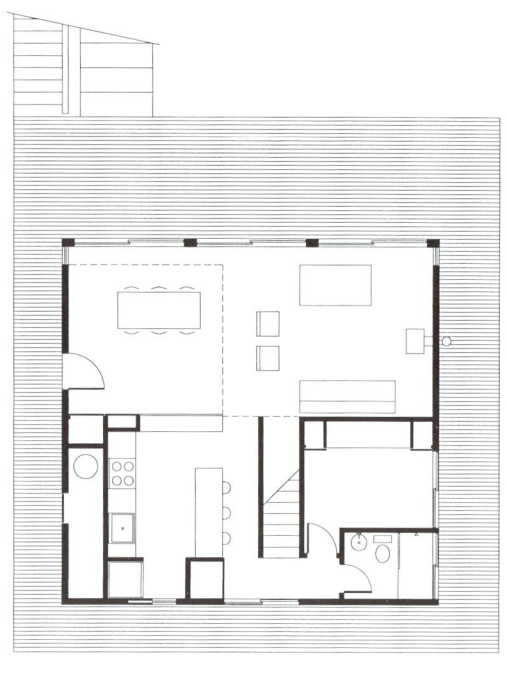
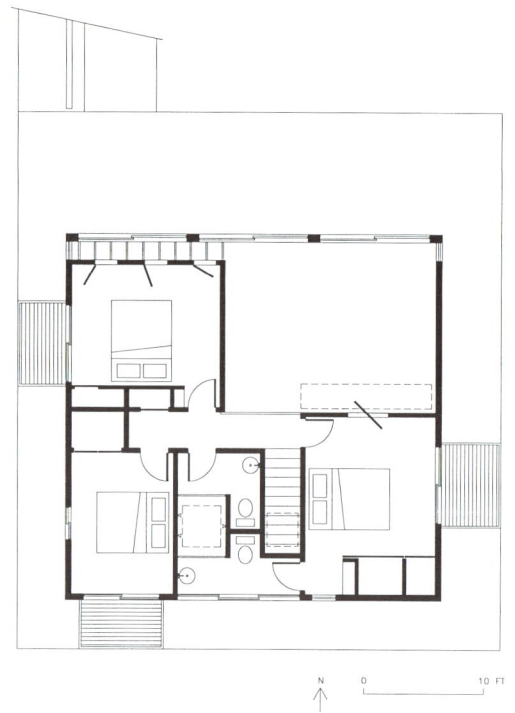

Ground floor plan

First floor plan

From the living room one can observe the pool and the orange-coloured wall that separates it from the path that gives access to the dwelling. A wooden deck surrounds the pool and covers the terrace that extends into the interior of the house. The contrast of colours and textures brings dynamism to a space of essential geometries and decorative minimalism.

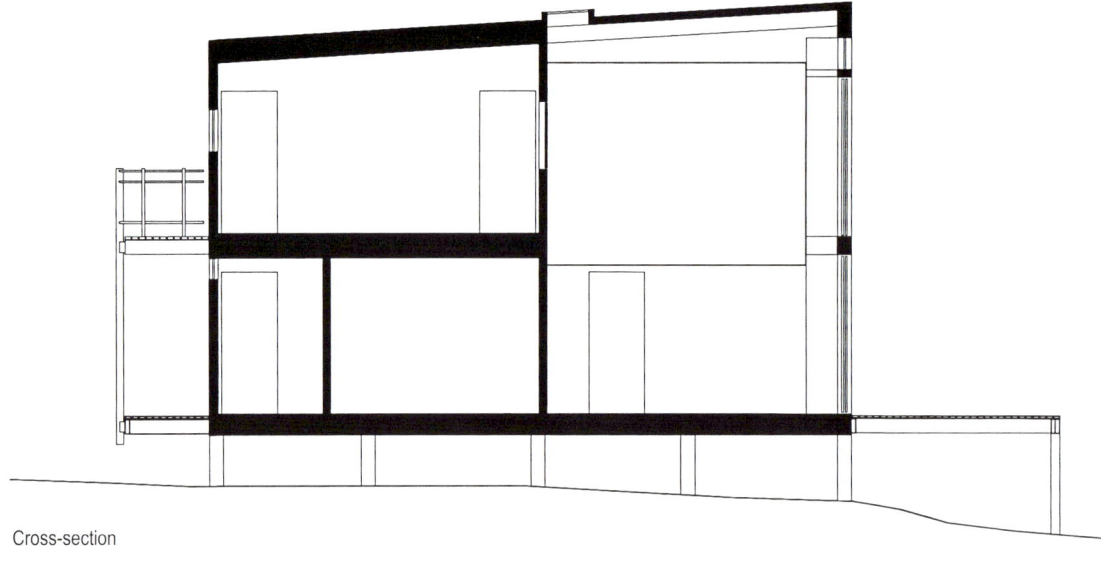
Cross-section

The solutions used in this dwelling are of great simplicity. The showers of the ground floor bathroom have double access, from the inside and the outside, thus connecting the two spaces. The connection between environments is a constant in this project: the dining room and the kitchen are separated only by a cloth screen. The kitchen includes a small, informal dining room. The highly minimalist lights used in this space help to create a sensation of functionality and order.

Will Bruder
Byrne Residence
North Scottsdale, Arizona

The sculptural design concept of this residence was to create a metaphorical series of abstract canyon walls of concrete masonry, emerging like geological landmarks from the home's natural desert site. As such, the home's architectural concrete masonry and metal-clad frame walls embrace the residence's main entrance, as well as its living and circulation/gallery spaces.

Furthermore, these walls highlight the angular geometry of the building's plan as it grows from the asymmetrical, tapering alignments of the canyon walls. These elements in turn visually extend the design out into the undisturbed natural desert site, creating interesting outdoor living spaces and courtyards.

The house is incorporated into the natural slope of the site's north-east corner, allowing the building's basic functional needs to develop on two levels. As it is placed on the site, the lower level is buried into the grade with a primarily south-western view exposure. The angular orientation of the structure, running parallel to the natural site contours, enhances the relationship with the terrain, while optimizing the distant view opportunities of all the living spaces on the main level. The tilted and leaning orientation of the masonry canyon walls serves to dramatically frame the site's distant desert vistas as one moves though the structure.

Only simple concrete block walls, treated as a dynamic sculptural element, could capture the potential of this architectural concept. Laid at a three-degree slope from the horizontal concrete foundations and leaning at varying angles from vertical, the beautifully crafted masonry walls are ever-changing in the desert sun. With the daily and seasonal variations of shadows playing off the subtle coursing offsets together with the buff-coloured masonry and the angular alignments of the plan geometry, the architecture possesses a mysterious quietness and power in the landscape. With a view to maximize these effects, the main roof is raised 4" above the supporting wall by skylit sculptural steel brackets which allow the sun to energize the interior as well.

Carefully balanced by vertical walls of masonry, metal and glass, the house exists as a poem of particular invention and originality. To complement the contrast with the dominant concrete masonry wall of the design scheme, wall and fascia elements are clad in blue/blackened copper and acid-etched galvanized metal. These materials, with their purple/bronze and pewter hues, will blend well with the natural landscape and the buff CMU. Completing the exterior palette is a glazing of clear and "solex" green non-reflective glass, set in custom configuration and details. The scale, sculptural form and the simplicity of its materials make the Byrne Residence an organic architectural statement that blends with and enhances its unique desert setting.

◧ Bill Timmerman

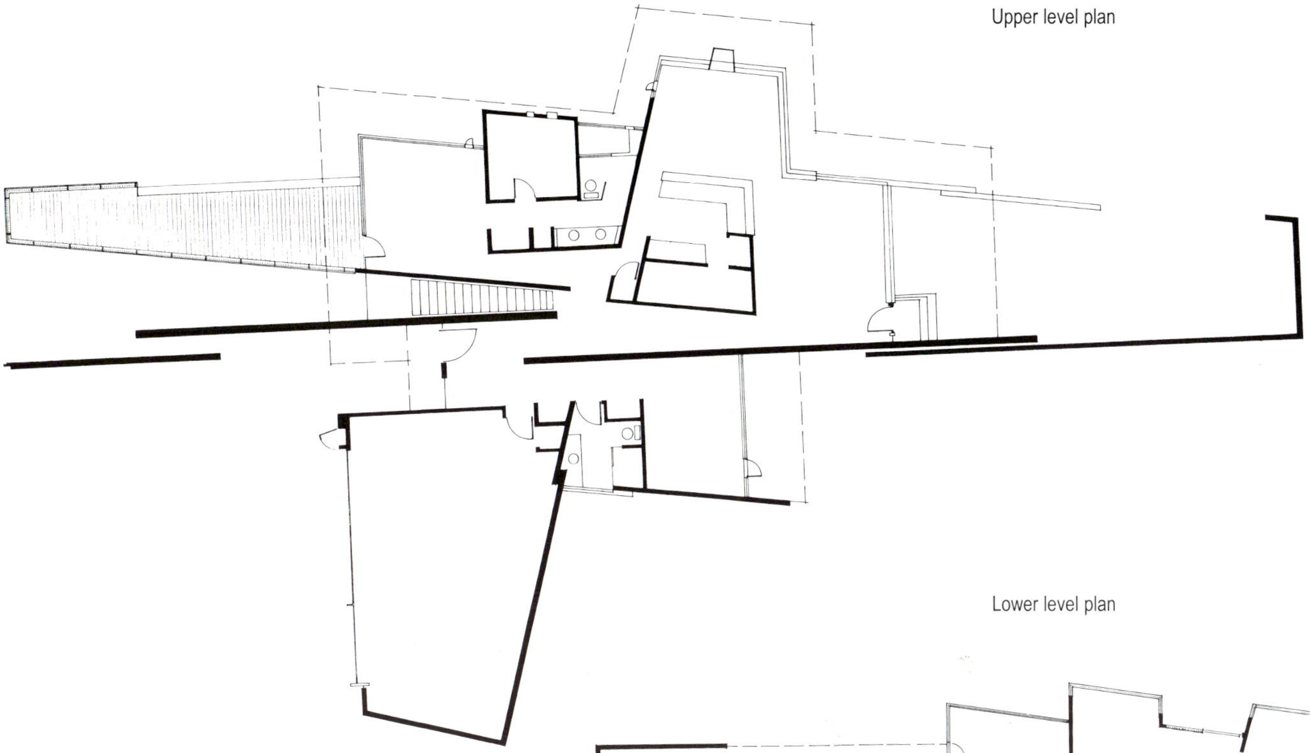

Upper level plan

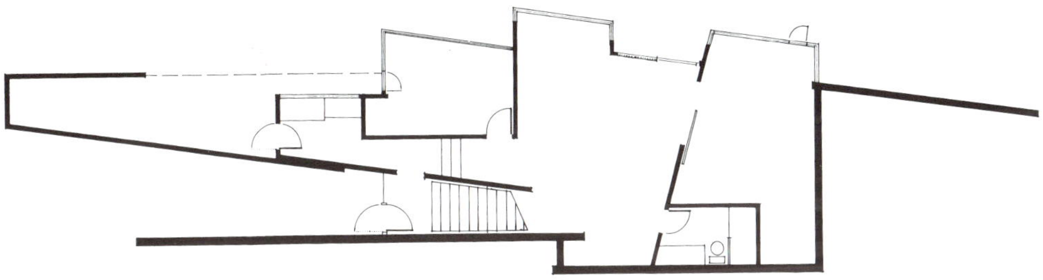

Lower level plan

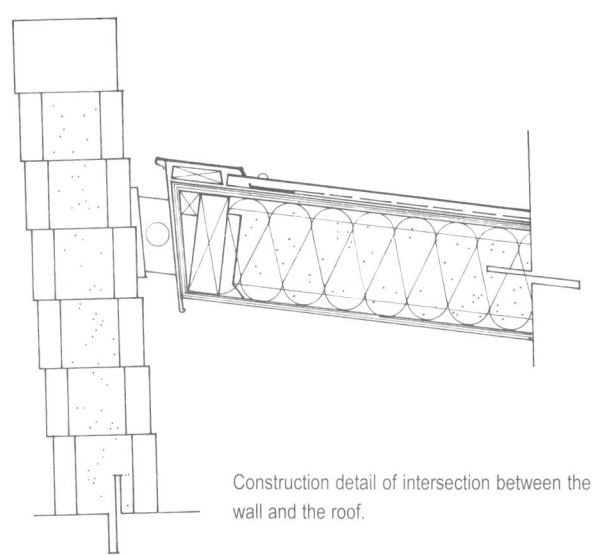

Construction detail of intersection between the wall and the roof.

Given the characteristics of the site of the dwelling, a desert landscape in Arizona, it was fundamental to achieve a complete mastery of natural light. It was not a question, as in other cases, of maximizing the light but of being able to graduate it according to the needs of the inhabitants. The careful placing of the windows and an emphasis on top lighting transform the interior of the dwelling into a very intimate and welcoming space.

The selection of the materials, with their constrasts of color and texture, shows the eclectic spirit that dominates the design. The different interior claddings, including wood, and metal (corrugated plate, galvanized metal) and the concrete walls and glass used on the exterior reinforce the idea of the house not only as an inhabitable environment, but also as a sculptural element.